Unseen Tears

———

The Challenges of Orphans and Orphanages in China

Beau Sides

Endorsements for Unseen Tears

"'Unseen Tears' is a wonderful and wholesome book that reminds readers about the affirming power of human goodness. The sweetest parts of the story center on orphans with special needs and all the lessons they provide everyone around them. 'Unseen Tears' is a story of love, compassion, and personal leadership."

Bill Treasurer, author of *Leaders Open Doors*

"Beau has done it again - his writing has given us a beautiful glimpse into the people and places of China. This powerful story about China's orphans will move your heart and call you to be a part of making a difference in the world. If you want to expand your understanding of China, read this book!"

Randy Gravitt, co-author of FINDING YOUR WAY: *Discovering the Truth about You*

"There are so many current world events that are loud and chaotic, demanding our attention. Yet Beau's book 'Unseen Tears' re-focuses our attention on a group of children who are quietly hidden away but desperately needing our attention. With his first person account, this book touched my heart for the disabled children of China."

Linda Pulley Freeman, author of *Thrive!* and *Inspired for Greater Things*

"Beau's book accurately depicts the life and challenges of being an orphan in China and also shares the plight of special needs orphans. Global Partners in Life (GPiL) is helping to meet the needs of these special children and give them opportunities that they would have never had... food and clothing, operations, schooling, and helping those that can work be educated to be a productive part of the Chinese society. I have seen first-hand that GPiL is making a difference in the lives of the children in China."

Leslie Sjurseth, Orphanage volunteer

"*My experience with China began in 2006 when I packed my two bags and moved to an unknown land and began teaching and serving in places I would have never dreamed. This book shows the huge need for ever-growing special needs population in China to be loved and adored just like any other child in the world.*"

Jennifer Bowden, Orphanage volunteer

"*Very honest and compelling account of the lives of orphan children in China. This book tells the story of the little lost lives living in China's orphanages. Truly an eye-opening piece of work.*"

Tammie Adams, Orphanage volunteer

"*Each child at the Home of Joy in China has left an imprint on our hearts. One has come to our home, but the rest of her family, at The Home of Joy, need continued help, physically, spiritually, nutritional support, financial assistance, and most of all our prayers.*"

Robin Cronin, Adoptive parent

"*I am thankful for the day that I heard the story of the children in an orphanage in China. Although the children change as shared in the amazing story of 'Unseen Tears,' the needs and tremendous medical challenges for the children remain the same! I am thankful that Beau has shared the story of these unforgettable children so their story might be forever in your heart! Beau has made a difference in my life and certainly in the lives of many, many children and others...you too can make a difference!*"

Brenda Clifton, Volunteer in schools and orphanages worldwide

TABLE OF CONTENTS

FOREWORD
BY MARK MILLER

Author Of Chess Not Checkers
And Co-Author Of The Secret

What breaks your heart? Perhaps you've never asked this potentially life-changing question. If you are open to ask and answer it,
the implications could be staggering. Beau Sides found his answer
over a decade ago when he founded Global Partners in Life.

I was with Beau and others on his first trip to China. We were
all moved by the kindness, hospitality, and generosity of the people we met. Beau experienced all this as well; however, he was not
just moved by our encounters, he was changed.

Human need has a way of doing that. When viewed honestly,
the needs of others can change our perspective on the world as we
see it. Beau was willing to take a step – towards the needs he saw.
He was determined to make a difference. That's why he is one of
my heroes.

When Beau took those first steps of faith, he was not aware
of the needs he would someday describe in this book. He wasn't
responding to a future need – he was responding to the present.
He was willing to do what leaders do – they respond with courage

in the face of complexity and uncertainty. He was not paralyzed by the unknown; he was empowered by the known.

Over the last decade, Global Partners in Life has cast an ever-expanding net of compassion to the people of China. This has been due, in part, to Beau's leadership, and in part, to the continuing discovery of virtually endless needs.

In the midst of this sea of need, Global Partners in Life has found a niche – an underserved group. Around the world, men, women and children with special needs are often forgotten. As a parent of an adult son with significant mental disabilities, I can speak to the reality and magnitude of the needs in America. Beau helps us all understand the same needs exist in a nation halfway around the world – perhaps more acutely as their nation struggles to modernize and serve more than a billion people.

In Unseen Tears, the names have been changed, but the people are real. You will sense this as Beau avoids the temptation to just tell a story; rather, he chooses the more powerful path – he takes us there. As you read his description of the people, places, and circumstances his friends encounter on any given day, be prepared to be transported there, to meet extraordinary people, to be changed.

-- Mark Miller
Vice President for Leadership Development, Chick-fil-A

1

AGAIN

I was excited to be in front of my computer, searching the internet for the best price for my upcoming flight to China. This trip would be very different from my first, taken just a few years prior, when I went as a recent college graduate to teach at a university. This time I was going to China, not as Jan Cross the college professor, but as Jan Cross the tourist.

My first time in China was the best experience of my life, and with it I accomplished my goal of becoming more connected with others and less fiercely independent.

Growing up as an orphan in the Mississippi foster care system had impacted me in several ways, not all of them good. Through endless relocations from foster home to foster home, I endured hardships no child should have to endure, and knew the pain of being a little girl growing up in abusive or indifferent environments. I learned quickly to discern which foster parents opened their homes because they loved children, and which ones did so only because they received a monthly check for their services. Being at the mercy of such an imperfect system inevitably instilled in me a strong desire to be in control of my own future.

The challenges I encountered within the foster home system gave me the determination to become educated, independent, and successful, and I refused to let anything or anyone crush my dreams. I enrolled in college immediately after high school graduation and worked as many as three jobs at one time to pay for my tuition, housing, and books. Between work, classes, and study time, I didn't have as much time to socialize as most college students do.

When we had group projects in school, my friends and classmates told me I needed to lighten up, because I oversaw how people performed their assigned tasks and wasn't shy about prompting them to complete their work on time and prepare for our meetings. I guess I just didn't have time to babysit, and I didn't want someone else's performance to affect my grades negatively, so I tried to be aware of everyone's progress and contributions.

I accepted a teaching job in China because I realized that I had become too controlling for my own good. I knew I would be a better and happier person if I changed, so I decided that the best way to alter my behavior would be to put myself into a situation where I had to rely on others. When I first arrived in China, I couldn't do so much as get something to eat without assistance from someone because I lacked the language skills. Additionally, I depended on the university for my apartment and everything related to my daily life. Relying completely on so many people was awkward and humbling for me, but it was exactly what I needed.

As I depended on and trusted so many people, I developed many fantastic relationships, and I am still in touch with the friends I made while there. I also hear from my former students and they still call me "teacher," which delights me. Their initial questions tended to be about things like English grammar, but now they ask for advice on their personal lives.

My adult friends from China are all connected in one way or another to the university where I taught. One of these is Canyon, whose wedding was the occasion of this latest trip—my second journey to China. Canyon and I were best friends when I worked at the university. We watched movies together, went shopping, and even climbed a mountain in her hometown. She was a huge help when I got into trouble with the dean for not using the curriculum provided by the university.

I had preferred to use my own material when teaching classes rather than resorting to the curriculum offerings. Dean Zhong took my insistence on using my own material so seriously that he told me he could fire me and put me on the next plane home if I didn't use the correct curriculum. My friends helped me think through what to do next, and Canyon did some research to help me prepare for a presentation I made to Dean Zhong. During that presentation and the meeting that followed, I learned that the curriculum he wanted me to use would help the students perform better on the standardized tests, so in that regard I was hurting my students instead of helping them by using my own material. I was, however, able to demonstrate how the students had improved in other areas, which Dean Zhong appreciated. Additionally, I was able to show the dean that the material I used was available for free on the internet, and he liked that as well.

Dean Zhong was very fair and patient in dealing with me. Rather than being angry, he was like a mentor teaching me what I didn't know or understand about the educational system of which I was now a part. Thankfully, he found room to compromise and use both types of material, and he allowed me to stay. I was grateful for his patience and wisdom to work through the mess I had made, and for everyone who helped me, including my friend Canyon.

The situation with the dean caused some embarrassment for me with Mr. Zao, the Director of Foreign Affairs who had recruited me. Going to him for advice when I had gotten myself into trouble was humbling. Fortunately, he wasn't upset with me, and he knew the system and Dean Zhong very well, so he was able to give some valuable advice. I grew very fond of Mr. Zao, and I enjoyed our conversations. He had been to the United States several times, and was trying to establish sister-relationships with other universities around the world. He was leading the way in sending local students abroad, while also increasing the number of foreign students on campus. Although we don't communicate often, I considered Mr. Zao a lifelong friend.

Undoubtedly, the two people from the university with whom I communicated most frequently were my dear friends Lizzy and Holly. Lizzy, an American and the Assistant Dean of the Foreign Language Department, had been my boss, but she never let me feel like she was. She always gave me so much information about the university, culture shock, and China in general, I would have embarrassed myself on multiple occasions without her guidance. Holly, the former Dean of the Foreign Language Department, should have been the unofficial mayor of the city because she knew everyone in town. It was wonderful for me that she still lived on campus because I often went to her for advice and information (and she is also a fantastic cook). Although Holly was Chinese, she spoke English with a British accent, which I assumed she had picked up as a child from her UK-born grandmother.

One topic that dominated my communications with Lizzy and Holly was the group of orphans that we and some of the other foreign teachers began providing for, after their parents died in a fire in an illegal fireworks factory. These orphans lived in a very rural area, about an hour-and-a-half drive from campus. One of my students had told me about the horrible event that led to them becoming orphans, so Holly and this small group of foreigners pooled our resources and raised some support for the children (who had been taken in by family members and local villagers). Thankfully, we were able to pay for their school fees and school supplies so they could continue their education.

Collectively, those of us who donated funds for the children agreed to continue providing support, and so far we had kept our agreement. In fact, our ongoing connection with them was one of the reasons for my returning to China, along with wanting to see my friends again. I had been back in the States for a while getting started on my career in publishing, but I wanted to check up on our little friends and see how we could better help provide for them.

Holly and Lizzy had partnered with a government organization similar to a ladies auxiliary, who kept them updated on the children's welfare and home environments. However, the organization lacked the resources to be able to financially support the children. This was where we came in.

One time, we went to the town where the children lived and visited a school. We met the principal and some local government officials, and then were surprised to be honored with a special program. The school band came out wearing full uniforms and performed in the sweltering heat. The orphans we supported were sitting in the front rows, and we sat with our fellow foreigners on the stage in the hundred-degree heat with no shade and no breeze. I didn't understand a word that was said during the speeches portion of the program. Later we got to meet the orphans we were supporting.

The opposite weather conditions existed last winter when Lizzy, Holly, and a few friends went shopping for the children in the wind, rain, and snow. The ladies auxiliary-like organization had arranged for a bus and driver, and they went to an open air market known for cheap dry goods to get coats, hats, gloves, and socks for the children. They even had enough money left over to give a small financial donation for food to the families who had taken in the children.

Another reason I was very excited about the latest trip was that Holly had been telling me about another local orphanage where she had been volunteering. She had grown quite fond of the children and of Anne, the manager of that orphanage. Holly knew about my background as an orphan, so she had been telling me all she could about the children and their backgrounds. She shared some moving stories about her time with them, so I was greatly anticipating meeting them soon. Holly also spoke highly of Anne, her service and commitment to the children, and her willingness to nurture them and stand up for them. Apparently, Anne had given up a successful career to provide for these children, and I looked forward to meeting her.

2

THE REUNION

I had prepared well in advance for this trip, and my boss had approved my plan for doing my reporting work while on the road, so I was ready to go. My flight to Beijing contained no surprises or delays, which was wonderful because I needed to catch a connecting train to reach the city where the university was and where the wedding would be held. I was very excited about seeing my friends, especially about seeing Canyon and attending her wedding. In fact, Canyon had said she would meet me at the train, though I didn't know how she would have time to do so this close to her wedding.

"Aaaaahhhhhhh!" A high-pitched scream pierced the buzz of the train station, but at first I didn't see why. Then there was Canyon, running toward me with her arms extended and an enormous smile on her face.

"You will never know how thrilled I am to see you!" I shouted.

"And you will never know how happy I am to see my friend from America!" Canyon's enthusiastic hug almost knocked me over.

"You haven't changed at all," I told Canyon.

"Neither have you!"

"So, tell me about this lucky young man who is going to be your husband! Don't leave out anything, from how you met to all of your wedding plans."

"Well, let's keep moving so we don't become a human traffic island."

"Okay, but you are not getting off that easily without telling me your wedding plans."

"No problem," Canyon said, laughing. "I enjoy talking about my 'Mr. Right' and our plans. We actually met through the university! He is a professor of Computer Information at another university, and his department needed some documents translated, but his university was only for technology so they didn't have an English Department. So, they came to our university and asked for assistance, and I was chosen to work on the project. We ended up working closely together because he was my point person for questions and issues. We began dating during the project, fell in love, and now we are getting married!"

"So, did you let him have any input into your wedding plans?"

"Well, there are a few cultural differences between the Western marriages you might be used to and Chinese ones, so some things our customs dictate," Canyon explained. "But to answer your question, I always give him my suggestion before I ask him for his advice. So far, he has agreed with me on almost every decision."

"You're smart to put it that way, and he's wise to go along with your suggestions. This marriage could work out very well for you if he continues to do that. It sounds like he has potential to be a great Mr. Canyon."

"Ha ha, 'Mr. Canyon,' listen to you!" Canyon laughed. "You make it appear as if I am the queen and he is my loyal subject."

"Well, isn't that how you want it?"

When we stepped outside, I saw that Canyon had already engaged a driver for us.

"A driver!" I objected. "Oh please tell me you didn't spend money on a driver for us! I thought we were going to take a bus back to the campus."

"Well, I have a little surprise for you." When Canyon opened the sliding door on the large black van with tinted windows, I heard old familiar voices shout "Surprise!"

For a second time, I almost fell backward. There in the van were my dear friends Holly and Lizzy! Shocked and speechless by this wonderful surprise, I left my bags on the pavement and climbed into the van, where we had an emotional group hug. I started crying and said, "I didn't know if we would all ever be together again, and now I see that you have gone to so much trouble and taken so much time to meet me. I am stunned, honored, and thrilled."

Holly explained, "We knew you were coming to China for the wedding, and we selfishly wanted to have time with you before it consumed all of your time."

The driver loaded my luggage into the rear of the van and began to drive. As I got comfortable in the seat, with Canyon beside me and Holly and Lizzy in the row in front of us, I couldn't resist taking in the scenery and atmosphere.

"Wow, the air seems cleaner than I remembered."

"The government has implemented countless programs to improve our air quality," explained Holly. "Some say that the new initiatives have had little impact, so it is encouraging to hear you say you can tell a difference."

"I can't believe I am getting to hang out with my dear friends on the way back to the campus where we all met! We have so much catching up to do. Tell me about what has been going on in your lives since I returned to the States."

As we talked and laughed, the driver sped us toward our destination. He never made a sound, unless he was answering a question or unscrewing the lid on his container to enjoy some cha, the ubiquitous Chinese tea.

Finally, the driver pulled up to the gated entrance of the campus, and Holly rolled down her window and spoke to the guard. He opened the gate and motioned for us to enter the campus.

"Thanks for arranging my reservation at the campus guest house," I said. "I don't know how I could have done it without you. Is the enormous container of tea with the snake in it still in the main dining room?"

"Yes, and they have another container of tea with a turtle in it," replied Holly.

"I also love eating the fried pumpkin patties from there. Hey, can I treat everyone to lunch in the dining room tomorrow? Canyon, if you invite Mr. Right, I will finally have an opportunity to see if he is good enough for you."

"Thanks for the offer," Canyon replied, "but you are going to be helping me prepare for the wedding tomorrow. As far as your meeting my Mr. Right, I will have to inquire about his schedule. Joseph, the English name I gave him, is excited about meeting you, and he wanted me to relay that you are welcome in our city and home anytime. By the way, Mr. Zao and Dean Zhong both said to please come by their offices while you are in town. They would love to say hello to you."

"Wow, I am pleased to hear that they remember me."

"Oh yes," Canyon said, "we speak of you often in the Foreign Language Department. Mr. Zao wants us to recruit people that have your energy level, and Dean Zhong says that you were his teacher and got him to think more globally and be more intentional about infusing more technology into our programs."

"That is so flattering! For a while there I thought Dean Zhong was going to fire me, and I knew Mr. Zao had to be mad about that. It couldn't have looked good for Mr. Zao since he recruited me."

When we reached the guest house, Canyon helped me check in. At first I thought I had lost my passport (which was required to check-in, as was standard practice in China), but finally I found it in my purse and paid for the room plus a security deposit.

As an employee led us down the dimly lit hallway to my room, we could see into some of the rooms whose doors had been left open. "Wow, the rooms have been nicely remodeled since the last time I saw them," I commented. Before, they had been dark and overcrowded, with nowhere to walk or place luggage or belongings. Now they had fewer beds, brighter lighting, and a fresh coat of paint on the walls and ceilings.

"It was all done for your return," Holly joked.

We entered my room and gave it a quick inspection. "Remember, you have to insert your room key into the slot on the wall for your room to receive electricity," Lizzy reminded me.

"Oh, that's right. I had forgotten about that. Perhaps I should return more often to keep my traveling skills at an acceptable level."

"We'll leave you alone because we know you're tired from your trip," Canyon said. "We've put some of your favorite snacks in the refrigerator, so you should be able to make it through the night. Will it be too early for me to pick you up at eight o'clock in the morning? We should get our day started reasonably early."

"Sure, that sounds like a wonderful plan to me. I will have eaten breakfast by the time you pick me up, so I'll be ready to go. How about if I meet you in the lobby?"

"That would be wonderful! Have a good rest, and I'll meet you there at eight."

As soon as the door was closed, I began to feel the fatigue from the long trip. Quickly I set the alarm clock, because I knew I was ready for a long night's sleep.

3

WEDDING CUSTOMS

The next morning I was up early and full of energy for a big day of helping Canyon with the wedding. It was only six o'clock, but it was already light outside (all of China has only one time zone—Beijing time—so depending on where you are, you can experience very early mornings or very early nights). I enjoyed some of the Chinese snacks my friends had left for me in the room, and I drank some of the delicious sweet peach juice that came in a wax paper-like container. Savoring these favorite local foods made me wonder why I had left China after my first visit.

Because I was ready for the day, I walked down the hall toward the stairs and was reminded that the lights work on sensors and don't turn on unless triggered by movement. As I entered the lobby, I could see the very busy street outside and noticed how much construction had been completed since I was last there. All of the trees that had been in the middle of the road were now gone, and the road itself had been widened and repaved. As I waited in the lobby, I couldn't resist looking at the display of refrigerated food, where you could select what you wanted for your meal. Many wonderful memories of enjoying meals there with students and friends came rushing back. I smiled and felt a great surge of warmth and energy.

I had to go look on the check-out counter to see if the huge jars of tea were still there. To my surprise, they had been removed. Maybe drinking tea with reptiles in it was no longer popular.

The lobby of the guest house had been remodeled, and the new furniture was big and overstuffed. The entrance was now all glass, so much more sunlight could enter, making the entire facility appear newer, cleaner, and larger. Through the lobby windows, I could see that the old man who repaired bicycles still had his cart set up on the corner. So did the vendor who carved pineapples into beautiful shapes and put them on a stick to sell to pedestrians— but now he had competition from vendors who offered students low-priced breakfast options. There were many breakfast choices near campus, and I remembered enjoying something that looked like an English muffin stuffed with lettuce, some type of meat, and an egg. Perhaps the most common breakfast for the students was hot soy milk, which they would hold in a clear baggie and drink with a straw, but I had never tried that myself.

As I was enjoying the ever-changing view and wonderful memories, there was a tap on my shoulder.

"Are you day-dreaming?"

"Hey Canyon, guilty as charged. You caught me thinking about all of my fond memories from here."

"You look well rested. Are you ready to go?"

"Sure, and I did sleep well. Thanks for the snacks in my room. I remember us enjoying those as we watched DVDs in my apartment. So what is on our agenda for this morning?"

"Well, our first and most important stop is the wedding gown shop. I think you'll remember it. We used to window-shop there as we walked up and down the street near the new shopping area and our favorite restaurants."

"Heck yeah, I remember that wedding gown shop! So did they make a dress for you, or did you select one that was on a hanger? I also remember you told me that the name of the street was Jie Fang Lu, or Freedom Street, because of the legend that Mao marched his troops down that street while he was fighting for control of China."

"Wow, somebody has no signs of jet lag today! I am so impressed that you remember all that. Have you been taking some memory enhancing herbs like gingko?"

"You're funny. While we're on our way to the gown shop, can you tell me about the wedding customs here in China?"

"Sure," Canyon said as we climbed into a taxi. "We have a saying here, 'Shi Li gai feng su,' which means, 'This is our custom, but go ten miles away and they will have a different custom there.'"

"When I was teaching here, some of my students told me that there are still matchmakers plying their trade. Is that true?"

"Yes, it is true, and that is one of the customs I was going to tell you about. One way for a couple to get together is through a matchmaker, but honestly they are not used much anymore. I would say that the matchmakers' services are used more in the small villages than in the large cities, but they are still used a bit in the cities as well."

"Interesting!"

"We do have another, more commonly used way to find someone to marry, which is what happened with Mr. Right and me. We met, dated, and fell in love. I think that is common in most places around the world. How about you—have you found your Mr. Right?"

"You know, it seems like all I do is work back home, so I have no social life to speak of. Sorry to disappoint you!" I had another question. "Most older couples I see in China don't wear a wedding ring. Why is that?"

"You have always been so observant! Well, that is something else that is slowly changing in our society. As Chinese have additional discretionary income, the younger generations are picking up western traditions, such as having wedding rings—which are not part of traditional Chinese culture. The internet and Western movies also have brought about some subtle changes like this."

The taxi turned onto a familiar-looking street. "If my memory serves me correctly, we're almost there. I've always loved this street because it has so much diversity. One end of the street has small, old shops and trees lining the street, and the other end has a new shopping area with a movie theatre. It's like old world meets new world all on one street."

"I've never thought about it, but you're right. You really are observant."

Canyon asked the driver to let us out so we could enjoy the street scene while strolling the rest of the way to the dress shop. This also gave me time to learn more about wedding customs.

"Tell me about your dress," I prompted Canyon.

"Well, actually, that would be dresses."

"Wait, are you telling me that you are wearing more than one dress for your wedding?"

"Yes, it is common here. We wear a red dress for the first part of the ceremony, and then we change into a white dress. The red dress is a traditional dress, for good luck. You know we love the color red here; just look at our flag and you can tell that. The white dress is something we have borrowed from other cultures, but the purity aspect isn't as much the motivating factor as just appearing more cosmopolitan."

"Considering all the female students I had when I taught here, I'm surprised none of them ever told me about that."

"Perhaps that is because the average age for getting married here has increased. Your students were probably thinking about starting a career and becoming independent before they got married, which is different from their parents and grandparents. Two dresses isn't so many. Some women wear three or four different gowns."

"Why the need for all the dresses?"

"There really isn't a need for all of them, but it's the bride's day so she wants it to be special. As an example, let's say the wedding will be at a restaurant. When the guests arrive and are greeted, the bride will wear one color dress. There may be an MC hired to keep the ceremony progressing, so she may be introduced by the MC and a funny game or two may be played. If there is someone the couple wants to show honor to, they will be asked to read the marriage license. There will be a huge meal, and the couple will walk around to each table visiting with their family and friends. While they are at each table, they will be given gifts, traditionally red envelopes full of money. The bride may change into another dress during the meal or while the MC entertains; I have heard stories of brides changing up to four times during the ceremony. As people begin to leave, the family will usually stay and have another meal together, or go to a family member's home for a meal with just the family."

"Wow, I can see why a bride would want to employ an MC to entertain her guests if she is going to change dresses so many times! What did you mean about reading the wedding license?"

"In China we usually have two phases of getting married. The first step is getting the marriage license from the government, and the second is having the ceremony. Traditionally, the honor of reading the wedding license is given to a family member who is held in high esteem or to a superior from work."

"So when are you legally married? When you get the license or when you have the ceremony?"

"Well, there is some debate about that, but I think technically speaking it is when you have the marriage license. Some would argue that with me, so it is only my opinion. People of faith will say that you need to have the license and the ceremony, but they use someone from a church, not an MC, from what I am told. Honestly,

I have never been invited to a wedding where someone of faith is getting married."

"You know, it is relatively similar in America. We obtain a marriage license from the government, and then we can go before a justice of the peace to be married or we can have a ceremony. Traditionally there will be a ceremony at a church or a restaurant. So who is going to read your wedding certificate?"

"My brother is going to read our wedding license. We chose him because he and his wife have twins who have been a delight to our family. Twins are a great occurrence in a family; since we have the one-child policy, it is the only way a family can legally have more than one."

"I'm interested in all of this, but here's the shop. Let's continue this conversation after we check out your gowns."

"Agreed."

Canyon and I continued to address the items on her wedding to-do list, and then I learned that she had arranged for me to have dinner with some friends with whom I used to teach. After dinner, my friends and I watched one of our favorite movies on DVD. Of course, we had playful conversations and too many snacks, and I stayed up way too late, but I did learn some interesting secrets.

4

THE WEDDING

When the driver let my "teacher" friends and me out in front of the hotel on the day of the wedding, we were extremely excited about finding Canyon. Soon we were all hugging her, telling her how beautiful she looked, and what a beautiful day it was for a wedding. Everyone agreed that Canyon's groom was a fortunate man indeed.

I was surprised by how much makeup Canyon was wearing. She looked like a performer in a Chinese opera, so I worked up enough nerve to ask one of my Chinese friends about it.

"This is very traditional for us," she explained, "and it takes a very long time to have all of the makeup applied. We also have wedding pictures made weeks before the wedding, and the bride will have some pictures made with the traditional makeup, and sometimes pictures made without it."

"Canyon is so beautiful without makeup, so I'm surprised to see her looking so different. I think this is the first time I've ever seen her wearing any makeup at all."

"Canyon isn't doing this for herself. She's doing it to bring honor to her family. We do many things to honor our families at the wedding, like spending time speaking with them after the ceremony is over."

"Thanks for all of the information. See, you are even teaching on your day off!"

"That isn't teaching, that is just hanging out with my *lao wai* (foreign) friend and sharing about our different backgrounds. Work is rarely this much fun!"

Canyon hurried us along. "You should go to the restaurant now so you won't have any trouble getting a good seat. I am very happy *all* of you are here!" That touched my heart, because I knew the emphasis on the word *all* was directed toward me.

We quickly made our way to the banquet hall where the wedding ceremony would be held. There was a huge inflatable archway outside the hall, and a smaller one inside. I was impressed with the flower arrangements and with how shiny the tile floor was. I could look down and clearly see the ceiling reflected in the polished tiles. Everything looked immaculate.

The ceremony had a great combination of music, speeches, toasts, and of course an enormous amount of food. I was thrilled to finally see Canyon's handsome husband. She had done well for herself. I already knew he had a good job, but he also seemed to be very gentle. He helped Canyon with her long dress on the stairs entering the banquet hall, and he smiled at the children, who acted shy when he acknowledged them. I also enjoyed meeting the twins in Canyon's family. I had heard so many stories about how lovely they were, and they didn't disappoint.

I could feel the love in the room, and I was thankful to have the opportunity to experience it with all of my dear friends. I saw Mr. Zao and his wife and son. I asked Mr. Zao why his wife didn't sing a song, since she is a famous singer, and he said that his wife didn't know Canyon nearly as well as he did. Mr. Zao gave me the good news that his son, James, had applied to go to a university in America, and he had been accepted. You could tell Mr. Zao was very proud of James, who spoke English very well, though he was quite reserved that day. He was going to go to a university in Mississippi, so I cautioned him about how hot it would be in the summer. I also encouraged him to try fishing, which finally brought a smile to his face. James said that he would go to the best information technology university in Qingdao for his first year, and then he would transfer.

I watched Canyon speak to everyone at each table, and noticed that she spent the most time with her parents and her husband's parents. She began the evening in a lovely red gown, then changed to a brilliant white dress. She was beautiful in both gowns as her shiny black hair stood out against whichever color she wore. I was thrilled for Canyon, and I could look into her face as she smiled at everyone at each table and know that my friend was genuinely happy as well.

To capture the moment in my memory, I backed away from the crowd and went to stand by a huge glass wall to absorb the environment. I was so thankful I had come and had gotten to see so many of my friends. I enjoyed the panoramic view of the river and the city, then turned again to see the people who had been such an important part of my life when I lived in China. I could see a couple of tables full of my teacher friends: Mr. Zao and his family, Lizzy and Holly, and so many others.

After I took a picture with my cell phone, my thoughts began to swing from the joy, excitement, and glamour of the wedding to our plans for the next day. Holly and I were going to visit some of the orphans from the fire in the fireworks factory. I couldn't wait to find out what their lives were like now, and I wondered whether they would ever enjoy an event like Canyon's wedding.

5

MEETING WITH ORPHANS

On the morning after the wedding, I called Holly to see how plans were shaping up for our visit with the orphans. "Good morning, Holly. How are you today? Have you gotten enough rest after the big day?"

"Yes indeed, I have rested well," Holly answered cheerfully, "and it certainly was a lovely wedding. I am so happy for Canyon and Joseph, and I believe they make a very handsome couple. Wouldn't you agree?"

"I absolutely agree. Canyon was stunning in her dresses, and I'm so happy for her. She told me that she and Joseph are going to Hainan for their honeymoon, and they would be the first couple on either side of their families to even have a honeymoon."

"You know," Holly said, "honeymoons are becoming popular here in China."

"That's what I'm told. So what about you? Did you have one?"

"Ha! Darling, I was married so long ago most people in China didn't go on honeymoons. Back then having discretionary funds for traveling wasn't very common at all."

"I have heard you speak of travels around the world, so I think you have certainly made up for it!" I switched the subject back to the reason for my call. "Is everything ready for a visit with the orphans? Don't forget, I'm totally depending on you to translate for me!"

"I am always happy to translate for you," Holly answered. "When I last spoke with the ladies auxiliary leader, I learned that they had made arrangements for some of the children with the best grades to meet with us today. We will get to see one child from the elementary school, one from the middle school, and one from the high school. These students have been performing so well that they wanted to reward them by letting them come into town today, and they have some activities and gifts planned for them."

"That sounds wonderful. I can't wait to see their faces and how much they have grown. I kept all of the pictures from when we met the orphans that hot day when Lizzy made her speech at the school."

"Yes, that was an extraordinarily hot day, and I was proud of how well Lizzy spoke. She is a gifted orator. By the way, I wanted to let you know that we're meeting at a government building today, so don't be surprised if you're asked to go through security or if you see more people in uniforms than in other buildings you've entered."

"No problems with that, and thanks for the heads up. I think it's a marvelous idea to reward the students for their hard work, so I tip my hat to whoever thought of it. If you'll translate for me, I'll congratulate the children on their accomplishments and encourage them to continue studying hard. My education has certainly opened doors for me that wouldn't have been opened otherwise, and I was motivated not to stay in the foster home system a day longer than necessary. Don't get me wrong; I'm very thankful for those who opened their homes to me, but I'm thrilled to have a little more control and freedom now."

"I will make sure to tell the students about your background and development, and I'm sure they will find you to be a kindred spirit and that you'll motivate them."

"Thanks Holly, it is always wonderful being around you!"

As always, Holly had arranged for a driver. As we traveled toward the meeting place, my thoughts were full of memories about hearing news of the fire and meeting with my co-workers to provide support for the children who had lost their parents.

Inside the government building, we encountered no scanners, but there were several people wearing uniforms of various colors and styles. I am sure each uniform referred to a specific rank or role but couldn't discern what they were.

Several people were already in the conference room where we would be meeting. The room contained an overhead projector, a podium, and a very large and modern table with holes in it for running cables to laptop computers and other devices. The room was not illuminated very well, so I didn't know if that would be an issue for the photographer who was there. The walls appeared to need a new coat of paint, but that could have been partially due to the lack of light in the room.

Three of the women in the room rushed toward Holly to greet her. Holly introduced me to them, but I immediately forgot their names. I did, however, learn that they all worked with the ladies auxiliary. They directed us to the large table and invited us to sit down, then they served us some hot cha in paper cups that were not sturdy at all but were placed in small plastic cup holders with handles.

Holly and her friends from the ladies auxiliary chatted for a minute or two, then the students entered the room. The three children looked intimidated by the gathering. They sat down across the table from Holly and me, so we had an excellent view of their faces. The youngest one still looked a little sleepy, but the other two looked very much engaged with their environment.

I loved how innocent their faces looked, and it was especially rewarding when they would smile about something. Their clothes were old and worn, but clean and without wrinkles, and they all wore similar shoes: the bottom was like a sports shoe, and the upper portion was like a dark blue slipper. The youngest student was a girl, and the older two were boys. After the children were given some cha, the youngest started waking up a little. Her eyes opened wider, and she seemed to follow what was going on around her with more interest.

I must admit that I wasn't completely engaged with what was happening because I couldn't understand what Holly and the women from the ladies auxiliary were saying. So like the students, I was just soaking in all that was going on around me.

Finally Holly and the three ladies from the auxiliary turned toward me. Holly explained, "The ladies wanted to thank you not only for your continued support of the orphans, but also for traveling so far to follow up with them."

"Holly, please tell them I wanted to thank them for their continuous monitoring of the children. I appreciate all they have done for the students and the updates they have provided for the teachers who are supporting them."

"Yes, I will tell them, but I have already expressed my thanks to them as well."

Holly turned and spoke to the ladies, and they all smiled and said "Xie xie," which I did understand: it means thank you. One of the three ladies from the auxiliary was a little older than the others, but she seemed to have the most energy, and she seemed excited to have all of us there. She bounced around the room making sure everyone's cup of cha stayed full.

"The ladies want us to get to know the children a little better," Holly told me. "So they suggest we ask them some questions, and then the children wanted to ask us some questions. "

"Wonderful!" I answered. "Would it be possible for me to learn the children's names?"

Holly translated my request, and then she pointed to the youngest one, who said her name was Tian. Holly then pointed to the middle student, and he said his name was Meng. There was no need for Holly to point to the oldest boy, because he immediately followed Meng by saying, "My name is Leon."

"Wow Leon, you speak English. That is fantastic," I said. "How long have you been studying the language?"

Leon looked up at the ceiling, thinking, and he started to blush a little. Holly said something to help him along, and then he smiled as if he finally understood what I had said.

"Uh, three years."

"Very good, Leon, so how do you like the language?"

There was another awkwardly long pause before Leon replied, "No good. Too hard."

Holly and I both burst into laughter, and I replied, "That is exactly how I feel about trying to learn to speak Chinese."

Holly translated, and then Leon laughed as hard as Holly and I had. Holly told me that the ladies wanted us to speed along in our conversation because they had some activities for the children and some shopping to do for them, but they also wanted the children to have an opportunity to ask Holly and me some questions.

The children asked us some standard questions—our names and how old we were, and so on—and then Meng asked, according to Holly's translation, "Why do you help us?" I was surprised by the question, but Holly answered quickly in Chinese and then in English: "My husband and I feel so fortunate to have been in a position to have provided for our children and grandchildren, and we still have more than we need. So, when I heard about some children being in need, I felt moved to assist you. When I worked I was a teacher, so I wanted to make sure all of the children who lost families and were devastated by the fire were still able to get an education." Holly then made a gesture with her hand that let me know the children wanted to hear my answer as well.

I explained, "I was teaching English at the university when I noticed how sad one of my students was, so I asked her why she seemed so sad. She told me about the horrible fire, and I asked some of the other teachers if they had heard anything about it, and they told me it was even worse than my student had told me. Many of the foreign teachers got together and decided we wanted to help keep all of the children in school who lost their parents in the fire, so we took up a collection to help. We agreed that we should all continue to make contributions so we could make sure all of you had your school-related expenses paid for." Then I told them about myself. "Like you," I said, "I am an orphan. I never knew my parents, so all of you and your stories touched my heart deeply. I thought that in a way it was easier for me to have never known my parents, compared to how difficult it must have been for all of you to have known and loved your parents and then to have become orphans."

Holly translated, and the children and the ladies all gasped with wide eyes when Holly told them that I had never known my parents. The ladies and children spoke among themselves, and Holly told me that they were surprised to learn I was an orphan too. Apparently they had never considered the fact that orphans exist all over the world. After their conversation, Leon leaned back in his seat, gave me a thumbs up, and said "Cool," so I think we had begun to bond.

Knowing our time was limited, I told the students that I wanted to urge them to keep studying hard, to encourage the other orphans and help them however they could, and to be helpful around the homes of the people with whom they were living. Holly translated this for me, and I watched their faces. They all nodded in the affirmative, and I believe they were sincere. Holly asked the children to tell us about the people they currently lived with.

Tian said she lived with her grandparents, and so did Meng. Leon said that he lived with his uncle and aunt, and they had a son two years older than him, so he always had someone to talk to and play with, and someone to help him with his homework.

The women appeared to be preparing to leave. Holly explained to me what was going on: "The ladies are telling the children that it is time for them to go shopping, so they will leave us now. I'll tell them for both of us how much we enjoyed meeting them, and I'll thank the ladies for arranging the meeting."

"Thanks, Holly. Please tell the children they are very special to us and it was a thrill to see them again." I pulled out my camera and quickly scrolled through some pictures of the hot day when we met at the school, so they could see how much they had grown and changed. They giggled and spoke very fast about each picture, but I don't know what they said because Holly was saying good-bye to the ladies.

As they left, Holly gave the ladies an envelope with money in it that we had prepared for our visit. This was for all of the orphans we were supporting, not just the ones who had come to meet with us. Holly had made the intent of the contribution clear in earlier conversations when this meeting was being scheduled, so the ladies knew how the funds should be distributed.

Afterwards, Holly and I talked about how the meeting had gone. "Well that was an enjoyable morning, wouldn't you agree, Holly?"

"Yes, yes, indeed I would. I think it made a big impression on the children that you are an orphan also, and that you have come from so far away to assist them."

"Yeah, I assumed that when they all gasped a little, it was when you told them I was an orphan."

"You are correct. I didn't expect that strong of a response from any of them."

"Oh well, if it helps us grow closer then it's a good thing!"

"I agree. Now how about some lunch?"

"That sounds great to me! I will defer to wherever you suggest, because you always know great places to eat."

"Okay, I do happen to know of a restaurant near here that has some wonderful eggplant stuffed with sausage."

"That doesn't sound like a combination I would have thought of, but if you say it's good, I'm ready to try it."

It was a short walk to the restaurant, which had very ornate furniture and was filled with beautiful antiques. It wasn't very crowded, so we were seated and served quickly.

"We're in luck," Holly said. "Today they have the eggplant dish I told you about."

"Great, I'm looking forward to trying it."

"You know, my husband is an accountant at a meat processing company, and he told me that this restaurant does a special order for the sausage they use for this dish. They require special seasonings to be added to the meat, and they also want the meat ground especially fine."

"Now I'm even more eager to try this special dish! I thought your husband was more of an operations manager for the company."

"You're right, but he started out as an accountant there and his responsibilities seemed to grow and grow."

I returned to the subject of our visit with the orphans. "It was pretty cool to hear Leon speaking English today, wouldn't you agree?"

"Yes, of course it was! I'm proud of him for speaking it to a native-English-speaking person and with so many strangers around. Many students would be too embarrassed to try doing that, even if they spoke English very well."

"Holly, give me your perspective on this, since you are Chinese and live in the area. How do you think the children have fared since becoming orphans?"

"Well, the children we met today may represent the best-case scenarios. They were all taken in by family members, so we know they are in a loving environment with people they already enjoyed a high level of comfort with, and perhaps that has helped them to do so well in school. I'm afraid that some of the others may have had a more challenging transition, especially those who didn't have any remaining family and so were taken in by local villagers."

"Yeah, that's kind of what I was thinking too. I was sure the ladies from the auxiliary wanted us to see that we were having a wonderful impact on the lives of the orphans, so they rewarded the highest achievers and introduced us to the children who had transitioned the best. Honestly, I would have taken the same approach if I were in their shoes. When you went with the ladies auxiliary group to bring winter clothes to the children, did it look as if they were being well taken care of?"

"Let me put your mind at ease," Holly reassured me. "The children seemed nourished and happy. Their clothes weren't new by any means, but they had enough layers to stay warm. They seemed proud of their new coats and toboggans, but one of the younger children wouldn't put his new coat on because he said it was too cold to take his old coat off."

"Well I can certainly understand that! You know I struggled with the bitter cold here when I was teaching, so I completely agree with that child. I am so thankful to hear that the children seem to be receiving good care. I often catch my thoughts drifting to them, and I wonder if my list of concerns is valid."

6

OPPORTUNITY TO SERVE

Holly and I enjoyed our delicious meal, and talked more about her work with orphans. I asked her about an orphanage where she and Lizzy had been spending some time, since she had told me about it in her emails.

"Oh, there are some absolutely darling children there," Holly said, "and they have stolen my heart just like my own grandchildren have done. The orphanage is here in town, so traveling there is no problem at all. The lady who leads it is named Anne, and she is very nice and patient with the children. We have become good friends, and I have so much respect for her because she has opened her own home to help the children."

"I'm committed to continue supporting the orphans from the fire in the fireworks factory," I responded, "but I'd also like to learn more about the local orphanage you have been describing."

"Lizzy and I are going there tomorrow, and we would love for you to accompany us; would that work with your schedule?"

"Sure, that would be wonderful. How should I dress?"

"Just wear jeans, and if you'll meet Lizzy and me at the south gate of the campus, I'll have a driver take us there."

"That sounds like a great plan to me, just like ordering this delicious eggplant dish!"

For the remainder of the day, my thoughts were with the orphans we had just met. I spent the afternoon walking around campus and visiting my favorite places: the koi pond, the flower garden, and the "English Corner"—a gathering spot that held fond memories of my Chinese friends meeting regularly to practice their English. And just like old times, the basketball courts were extremely busy. I wondered whether all of the orphans from the fire were adjusting as well as Meng, Tian, and Leon. Were they encouraged and pushed to excel in school? Were they given enough to eat and provided with proper clothing? Did they have a warm place to sleep at night? How were they treated at school? I know far too well that orphans are often picked on at school. Hopefully that wasn't the case for these resilient children, since the fire had affected so many children in the town.

By the time I went to bed, I had peace within myself that although some of the orphans were probably doing better than others, as a group they were doing okay. Some were excelling, of course, and I knew that counseling had been provided after the accident, so I hoped that the children had an inner peace about their new lives and were making the best of what they had. It truly was wonderful to meet Meng, Tian, and Leon, and to know that they were doing well and that a special day had been planned for them. Perhaps the strength I saw in them gave me hope that the others were strong also.

That night I got a good night's sleep, since the mattress I slept on, like most mattresses in China, was extraordinarily firm. My back has never bothered me at all after sleeping on these hard beds. For breakfast I snacked on some of the dried fruit I had in the room, then did some writing for work. Thank goodness for laptop computers! For lunch I walked to one of my favorite mom-and-pop restaurants near the west gate of the campus. The owners can make mashed potatoes and gravy just like every grandmother in the States, so I like to get that and their fried green beans. Yep, I am a southern girl, and when I eat there all I'm missing is a tall glass of sweet iced tea.

As I walked back to my hotel, I knew I had time to do more work on my laptop, but I was becoming curious about what I might see at the orphanage Holly and Lizzy would be taking me to later in the afternoon. I wondered if I would see something that would remind me of my past, and I wanted to learn more about the leader, Anne, and the children.

The weather had brought a little rain the previous night, but the skies were very clear and blue when I walked across campus to meet Holly and Lizzy at the south gate. Fond memories surfaced one by one as I passed each building, and I often caught myself smiling broadly.

I was the first one to arrive at the south gate, then Lizzy and Holly arrived together. Holly waved, and out of nowhere a taxi pulled up beside her. "Holly," I exclaimed, "I don't know how you can consistently have a taxi just waiting to pick you up. I think you have taxi magic!"

Holly laughed. "Nonsense, darling, he would have come just as quickly for you. I have no magical powers over the taxis of our city."

Lizzy agreed with me. "Holly, I think Jan is correct. I've noticed on many occasions how fortunate you are in getting taxis quickly. You do have taxi magic!"

As we climbed into the taxi, I had another question for Holly and Lizzy. "Why do so many vehicles in China have a red cloth tied to the four wheels?"

"It's for luck," Lizzy answered. "The people of China are probably a little more superstitious than Americans, so they place the red cloth on their vehicles for good luck."

"That's a great idea. If I drove here, I would want good luck protecting my vehicle, and me as well!"

Just then the driver pointed to one of the funniest things I have ever seen. A street vendor had a small monkey and a small dog on separate leashes. The monkey held a stick with a red string on it that looked like a whip, and it was playfully using the make-believe whip to strike the dog. The dog would engage in a play fight with the monkey and take the whip away. The dog would then jump into the arms of the vendor, and the monkey would climb the vendor like a tree. After the pets had rested for a moment, the vendor would put them down and let them perform their theatrics again. If only I had thought to grab my camera! We laughed and made jokes about the scene all the way to the orphanage.

As we drove through the gated entrance to an apartment complex, Lizzy helped me get my bearings. "The apartment building on the left is the building where the orphanage is, and it isn't on the top floor, so you don't have to worry about waiting a long time for the elevators. Just follow us through the playground, and then we'll enter the building."

"Maybe we'll be able to bring the children outside to play," Holly said optimistically.

We entered the lobby of the apartment building and passed a man sitting in a small office area where he could see everyone going in and out of the building. I assumed he was some type of security guard, but I wasn't sure because he didn't wear a uniform. On the other side of the lobby was a set of elevators.

"We're lucky," Holly said. "A few years ago a law was passed requiring that any building being built with six or more floors needed to have elevators. This building has twenty-four floors, so it easily qualifies."

"How did people in tall buildings manage before the law was passed?"

"Not well, apparently. I've heard about people dying while they were walking up or down the stairs in the heat of the summer."

Lizzy nodded her agreement. "It really was a problem in the cities where it gets extremely hot in the summers."

The area of the lobby outside the elevators was poorly lit, but we could still easily navigate through the semi-darkness and press the number for our floor. We rode up, and the elevator opened again onto another poorly illuminated area, where a couple of bikes were parked and clothes were drying on a rack. I followed Holly and Lizzy as they turned a corner, and we saw vegetables piled on the floor next to the wall, another clothes rack, and a stairwell. Just before the stairwell was a door on the left. The door had a few plaques above it that I couldn't read.

Holly pressed the doorbell, and I could hear a commotion inside. The door opened, and as we walked in about fifteen children were standing with their arms raised and their hands motioning like a forest of giant sea kelp, waving for someone to pick them up. Thankfully Holly and Lizzy had entered in front of me because I didn't know what to do. There were too many children for the three of us to pick them all up at one time.

A lady came into the room, simply dressed in a skirt and a couple of layered shirts, with a soft-looking white shirt as the undermost layer and a denim shirt with some embroidery on top. She wore socks that were turned down once above her ankle, and simple slip-on soft-soled shoes. The children parted to let her walk toward us, and then she gave Holly and Lizzy a big smile, and Holly introduced me to her. This was Anne.

"Nice to meet you," Anne said in English with a Chinese accent.

"Nice to meet you too, Anne," I answered. "I've heard many wonderful things about the work you do with the children, so I'm thankful to have an opportunity to visit."

"We are always happy to have a new friend," Anne responded graciously.

I was desperately hoping that Holly or Lizzy would tell me what to do next because I was at a loss as to what to do or say. Holly and Anne started speaking in Chinese, so I just reached down and picked up one of the children who was standing there with outstretched arms. She was a darling little girl with huge, sweet, dark brown eyes. She giggled and gave me an enormous smile. My new little friend had two pony tails, one with a bright red clasp and the other with a bright yellow one. I bounced her up and down a little bit and turned in a circle slowly.

As I spun around, I saw that Holly and Lizzy had neglected to inform me about one critical piece of information: this was a special needs orphanage! I could see a couple of children in wheelchairs in another room, and some of the children had visible signs of medical issues and treatments, but that didn't dampen their enthusiasm or excitement.

There was a large, low table in the room, only about two feet off the floor, and Holly said we could put our things there. Also I saw a nice built-in shelf beyond the table that was used for storage. Surprisingly, there were a couple of mattresses on top of it. Beyond the shelf there was a partially glassed-in balcony with metal shelving on it that was being used to store anything and everything imaginable. I saw strollers, hula hoops, boxes, bikes, diapers, soccer balls, badminton rackets, and even a ladder. It looked like every inch of space was being used.

The child I was holding was pulling on my shirt, wanting more attention. I bounced her up and down again, and I was surprised by how light she was. She had on a cute pair of pants and a shirt with Snoopy from the comic strip Peanuts on it. I noticed that she, just like all the other children, wore socks and indoor slippers.

Off this entrance I could see a narrow kitchen with some pots on the stove-top, which ran on propane from a canister under the stove. I couldn't see very far into the kitchen, but I could see it was closed off without a connecting door to another very large room, which had ornate built-in book shelves and a large counter below a huge window that let in tons of light.

Lizzy motioned for me to come into the large room, and then I noticed how high the ceilings were. They had to be about fifteen feet high, and had beautiful crown molding the same shade of white as the ceiling. The floor was a worn laminate and could have used a good scrubbing. There was an arched doorway at the opposite side of the room. I couldn't see where it went, but I could tell that there were cribs near the window, which made it difficult to walk in that area. There was also a large white sofa with a cover over it; clearly, Anne wanted it to stay white.

An array of photos on the wall caught my eye: pictures of children of various ages, shapes, and sizes. I imagined that there was an interesting story behind each photo, and I hoped to learn these stories one day. Seeing these pictures took me immediately to my childhood of growing up in the foster home system in Mississippi. I had lived in over a dozen foster homes, and I don't think any of them had this many pictures. Some didn't have any pictures at all of the children who were living there or had in the past. As I bounced from home to home over the years, the presence or absence of pictures had helped me to tell which foster parents truly cared for the children and which ones did not.

"Today I brought some watercolors for the children to use to paint a picture," Holly told Anne. "Is it okay if we do that now?"

"Yes, sure. The children will enjoy doing that. I'll get some water, and you can get the children started." Then Anne said something in Chinese, and the children started clapping their hands together and jumping up and down. Some of them went to the entrance room and got small chairs and put them around a long, low table in the big room. Holly opened her bag and removed the paints and gave the children some paper for their activity. Anne brought in a few bowls of water, and the children grabbed their brushes and started painting. I couldn't believe how much quieter it became. It was as if the painting had cast a magic spell of silence on them. Soon enough, though, one of the children didn't want to share a tray of paint with the others, then the fussing began and the spell was broken.

This was an emotional moment for me, so I stepped back into the entrance area and watched the children while I regained my composure. This overwhelming new environment brought back so many memories.

I thought about how kind, caring, and loving Anne was to take care of the children, and I didn't know how she could keep doing it day after day. I wondered where all of the workers were who would be needed to provide the care required by so many children. I did know that the children were fortunate to have buddies like Holly and Lizzy to come and entertain them. When I was in foster homes, sometimes someone from a university who was majoring in social work would come to spend time with us, but that was about it.

Lizzy got up from her seat at the table, and she patted each child on the head as she walked past. She also said something to each child in Chinese. I don't know what she said, but it made each child smile, and that was all that mattered. Lizzy motioned for me to come with her. We walked through the arched doorway, and there in front of us was a huge picture of Anne, her workers, and many children. As I stared at the picture, Lizzy smiled and said, "Yeah, it's impressive, isn't it?"

"Wow, where did all of the children come from?" I asked Lizzy. "And how did they all stay still long enough for the picture?"

"Well, I'm sure it took more than one attempt with the photographer to get a good picture, but all of them lived here at the time," Lizzy answered.

"There must be close to twenty children here now. Where do they all sleep?"

"Come, and I will show you another large room."

We walked through a short hall beyond the arched doorway and into a very large bedroom. It must have been about twenty by twenty-five feet, and had very high ceilings. Like the other large room closer to the entrance, it had sturdy wooden bookshelves and a large window in the middle of the wall. There was a radiator covered by a countertop under the window. The room had several cribs, a set of bunk beds, and some brightly colored mats on the floor that resembled yoga mats but were a little thicker. The wooden cribs looked strong and well made, but they were worn, with paint flaking in a few places. Each crib contained at least one baby or very young child, and some cribs had two babies in them.

I am sure my mouth was wide open as I moved my head to get a panoramic view of the room. Lizzy interrupted my gawking: "Yeah, now you know why I wanted you to see this room."

"Lizzy, I would have never guessed that there were this many children here—and so young!"

"Oh, you will have multiple surprises here, and one is about to untie your shoe."

I looked down and saw that Lizzy was right. Sitting beside my foot was a small child I hadn't seen come in the room. She had one shoelace in her hand, and she looked up at me. I couldn't help but laugh at her sweet and playful face, and she started laughing too. Her little cheeks were plump, and her bangs were cut straight across her forehead, so her face looked very round. My new little friend didn't untie my shoe, but she did sit on it, so when I took a step she got a ride. I circled the room with her on my foot a few times and she was giggling the entire time.

"Well, looks like you've made a new best friend!"

"Yeah, Lizzy, we are kind of attached to each other!"

As I continued circling the room with the rider on my foot, I noticed large cabinets that were held together with cloth tied around the handles. Because the doors were bulging open, I guessed that the tied strips of cloth kept the contents from spilling out and kept the children from getting into the cabinets. I wondered about the challenges Anne must face trying to store everything with so many people living there. Luckily, this was a very large room; otherwise, there was no way so many children could sleep there.

My tour of the room with my little anchor friend led me past another door. On the other side was a room with a tile floor, and I could see three sinks, so I assumed it was the bathroom. Each trip past the door gave my nose an unwanted jolt, so I guess Lizzy was right again about surprises. I recognized the scent of a diaper hamper, an odor I recalled from a couple of the foster homes in which I had lived. As I looked back at the children in the cribs, I noticed that some of them had cloth diapers, but a couple of them were wearing disposable diapers. I was sure there was a logical explanation for the difference, but I couldn't tell what it was. Too bad I couldn't ask my little friend attached to my foot.

A very slight older woman with wavy gray hair and a caring look in her eyes came in and said something in Chinese to the little girl. She reached out and took my friend by the hand. I waved good-bye and the little one tried to hide behind the woman, then peeked between the older lady's legs, blushed, and waved good-bye to me.

Lizzy had left the room, so I was alone with the babies in the cribs. As I slowly walked around the room and looked at each child, I thought about touching them, but they were all asleep and I didn't want to wake them. I wondered why these babies were here and what possible reason there could be for their parents not wanting to be with them. I thought about how kind Anne was to take care of the children, and I wondered who took care of me when I was so small.

Lizzy came back into the room and asked me to come with her. She wanted some help putting up something like a clothesline to hang the children's paintings on. This way the children could admire their work and the pictures would dry more quickly. Holly helped the children complete their paintings, and then instructed them to bring their artwork to Lizzy and me near the entrance. It was fun to watch the children look at the paintings as we hung them. When the older lady with the wavy hair walked through the room, all the children wanted to show her their paintings.

After we had hung all of the pictures, Lizzy and I helped Holly and Anne clean up the mess from the watercolors. Thankfully, someone had thought to put a large plastic sheet on top of the table where the children were painting. The plastic sheet was thick and durable, so I knew it could be used often and cleaned and used again.

While Anne, Holly, and Lizzy spoke with one another in Chinese, I watched the children entertaining themselves. Some were playing cards, some were looking at books, some were just talking, and others were pushing and pulling on each other. The children played remarkably well together, considering that they were living in such tight proximity.

I also started noticing that some of the children's special needs were obvious, but some weren't. A couple of the children had scars on their upper lip, I guessed from surgery to correct a cleft palate. A few other children walked with an odd gait; I imagined that had something to do with their hips, legs, or feet. One thin boy lying on a bed off to the side of the room couldn't or wouldn't move much at all.

When the ladies inexplicably started speaking in English, I heard them making plans to return in the future, and Holly said she that had some books to bring them. Knowing Holly, I was sure the books would be educational. We collected our things and started heading toward the front door just as someone was knocking. Anne opened the door and in came a group of college-age people. The children went to them just like they had approached us when we arrived, with their hands in the air, wanting to be picked up.

Holly gently tugged on my arm and motioned toward the door. "This is a good time to leave, while the children are distracted," she said. She had gathered her things, so I put on my backpack and headed through the door.

I turned back and told Anne it was nice to have met her, and I thanked her for taking care of the children. "It is my pleasure," she answered, smiling, "and I hope to see you again."

"Thanks, Anne. You will see me again!" Before I turned away from the door, I could see the children already playing with the young group who had just gone in. We walked to the lobby area and waited for the elevator, and Holly asked, "Well, how do you like our little friends?"

"Oh they are absolutely darling! One was riding my foot as I walked around the bedroom with the cribs."

"That must have been Wang Wang. That's her favorite game."

"Holly, do you know all of the children's names?"

"Yes, I do, but it took me a while to learn them. It will be more difficult for you, since only a couple of them have an English name. You must have some questions for us about what you saw on your first trip to the orphanage, so go ahead and ask."

"You know, I do have lots of questions, but I may need to absorb everything first. Today brought back many memories and emotions for me, and not all of them were positive ones, so I think I will hold off on asking my questions. You know me—once I get started, I could go on for an eternity."

I put my hand on Lizzy's shoulder and suggested, "Since Holly is in a hurry to get home, I think we should ask her to use her taxi magic."

Lizzy laughed. "I absolutely agree. Holly, go ahead and use your magical powers to produce a taxi quickly."

"You two are being silly with the taxi magic, but I'll see what I can do." As soon as we passed through the gate to the apartment complex, we noticed a driver taking a nap in his taxi in the shade of a large tree. Holly went directly to him and said something, and then motioned for us to join her.

"Well done once again, Holly!" I congratulated her. "I think you must be an owner of the taxi company, and that is how you arrange these quick pickups!"

7

QUESTIONS

On the way home, I eagerly asked my friends, "Do y'all think we'll have an opportunity to return to the orphanage in the near future?"

"Darling, sure we can!" Holly answered. "Lizzy and I weren't sure how much you would enjoy being in that environment with your background, so we didn't want to push you into something that made you uncomfortable."

"Thanks for considering my feelings, but I enjoyed spending time with all of those precious faces. I can only imagine the stories Anne has to tell about them. So yes, I want to return."

"Well," Lizzy said, "Holly and I had planned to go there again tomorrow afternoon. Would your schedule allow you to join us?"

"Yes, I should be able to complete my work if I spend some time on it tonight and in the morning."

"Great!" said Holly. "Let's meet at the south gate, and we can take a taxi together."

The next day Holly worked her taxi magic again, and when we reached the apartment complex, I followed Holly and Lizzy to Anne's home. I think I could have found it on my own, but I wasn't sure, so I was motivated to be more observant on this visit. I asked Holly what the plaques above Anne's door said.

"That is an official license letting people know that there is an orphanage here and that the government knows about it, and has given its permission for the orphanage to be here. There's a long story about her license that I'll have to tell you over tea someday, but we don't have time now."

"Okay, I'll look forward to hearing about that." I truly enjoyed hearing Holly's stories, because she had the ability to provide tremendous amounts of information and make it entertaining.

As the door to the orphanage opened, we again encountered a wave of children wanting to see who had come to play with them, but this time there were not as many children as before. I asked Anne where the other children were.

"They've gone to school," was Anne's answer, and I was a little embarrassed that I didn't remember that our initial visit was on a Sunday.

"Today I brought some Play-Doh," Lizzy announced to Anne.

"Wonderful, the children love playing with Play-Doh. That is one item that gets used so much, it doesn't last long here. Thanks, Lizzy."

"Well, don't just thank me. Holly had to help me find it in a store, and Jan gave us the money for it, so it's a team effort. All I did was carry it!"

"Okay, thanks to all of you!" Anne said. "The children will enjoy playing with it today. Look, they've already put the plastic cover on the table and brought in some chairs."

"We'd better not keep them waiting any longer," I suggested. I picked up two small children who were standing near the entrance with their hands in the air and walked them into the large room with the short table. When I set the children down, they quickly found an open area at the table, and everyone scrambled to get some Play-Doh.

I thought it would be interesting to see what the children created. There was quite a buzz at the table as they energetically went to work. Initially it appeared that the older children had an advantage with designing their masterpieces, but the younger ones quickly caught up, and some even surpassed the older ones. The children talked among themselves as they went about their work. It made us all happy to see them smiling and playing so well together. It was amazing how such little effort on our part could bring smiles to the faces of our little friends, and I wondered if I was the same way at their age.

After a while, one little boy who had made small balls with his Play-Doh threw them at the other children. Then one of the older girls took some putty from one of the younger kids, so the fussing started. Anne came over and said a few sharp words, and then there was silence until the child whose Play-Doh had been taken started to cry. The children got along unusually well, but they were children after all.

After everything calmed down, Anne left the children to their play and sat beside me. I took the opportunity to ask a question: "Anne, who were all of the young people who came in as we were leaving yesterday?"

"Oh, those were students from some of the local schools. Some are college students, and some are in high school—or senior middle school, as we call it. The college students are mostly majoring in social work, and the senior middle school students go to a private school that has a couple of teachers who come here, so they try to bring some students when they can."

"It sounds like you have a nice system of support for the children."

"Oh, but we always need more help!" Anne said with a chuckle.

"I'm sure you do! I don't know how you manage to keep everything running so smoothly. The children are fed, clean, and loved. Those are the most important things."

"I have a dream of doing more for the children. One day I would like to have enough money to hire a physical therapist and a speech therapist. I also want to open a nursery school. We could use the proceeds from the nursery school to pay for the orphanage."

"Wow, you have some enormous goals! I'm impressed. I hope you can make all of that happen."

"Thank you!"

"Anne, would you mind if I ask you some more questions?"

"Holly and Lizzy told me you are a good person, so you can ask me any questions you want."

"I'm happy to know that my friends said nice things about me! My first question is why there are so many special needs orphans here?"

"You need to know a little about our history to understand my answer. When China implemented the one-child policy, it made people think differently about a special needs child. If you can only have one child, then you want it to be normal, healthy, and perfect—so sometimes people will abandon a child with a disability or condition."

"If the parents abandon the child, then they can have another child who will hopefully be normal? Do I understand this situation correctly?"

"Yes, that is the main reason the children are abandoned. But some parents abandon a special needs child because they know they can't afford to pay for the medical attention needed. They feel that the child will have a better chance if it is abandoned."

"I don't know if Holly and Lizzy told you this about me, but I was raised as an orphan myself."

"Yes, they told me, and they said you would be able to understand things from the children's perspective better than most people. They also said they think you will have a soft spot in your heart for the children."

"I don't know how well I will understand things from the children's perspective, but I definitely have a soft spot in my heart for them! So how do the children come to you?"

"The three main places the children come from are the hospital, municipal orphanages, and the train station."

"How do those places know to send children to you?"

"It would take too long to give you all of the stories about each group," she answered, "but I will give you the short versions. Over the years the hospitals have started calling me when a child is abandoned onsite. We have built strong relationships with the hospitals because I've been bringing children to them for treatment for so long. So when a special needs child is abandoned at some of the local hospitals, they will call me directly to come and rescue the child."

"That is impressive; they must truly trust you to call when a situation like that occurs."

"Thank you! And then the municipal orphanage will call me to take a child from them when there is a dire case or when a child needs an operation."

This puzzled me. I would have thought municipal orphanages would be better equipped to serve children with special needs. "I don't understand," I said. "Why would they call you for those situations?"

"Well, I have a long-standing relationship with the local municipal orphanage, and we try to help each other provide the best care for the children. If a child is struggling or not responding well in his or her environment, they will send the child to me. I am in a position to give more individualized attention. Sometimes there are just too many children at the municipal orphanage for the workers to provide all of the care needed. They try hard, but sometimes there just are not enough people and resources."

"Can't the government give more money to the municipal orphanages?"

"Well, everyone has a budget, so it's extremely difficult to get additional funding. Orphans aren't a big priority for the government's money. It is much more popular to build a new road than to increase funding for orphans. Don't get me wrong; people do want the orphans to be taken care of, but they want it to be done inexpensively, and they don't really want to see the special needs orphans paraded around by someone trying to raise support for them."

"What about the train stations?"

Anne lowered her eyes. It must have been difficult for her to talk about a child being left alone in a public place. She explained, "Parents who have decided to abandon a child sometimes choose to leave them at a train station because there are so many people there, and the parents know the child will be found quickly and start receiving care."

"Oh my gosh! I can't imagine placing my child on the cold concrete floor and walking away!"

"If you remember," Anne reminded me, "we talked earlier about how some parents know they can't afford to provide the medical care their children need, so they abandon them in hopes that the children will receive that care from whoever finds or ultimately takes them in."

"That just seems too sad for words to describe."

"Yes, I understand your thoughts on that, but some of the parents would say that they do it because they love their child, and this is the only hope they have of getting the necessary medical attention."

"That's very hard for me to get my mind around. Let's change subjects. Since you mentioned funding, how do you manage all of the expenses you incur with all of these mouths to feed? I hope you don't mind me asking."

"It's okay to ask. Our largest contributions have been coming from an international church in Hong Kong. We also have a successful businessperson who is generous to us. He adopted one of the children from here, and they now live in Australia. The church he attends supports us too, so we are very thankful for both."

"What about local churches—do they give you support?"

"They do give us a little," Anne said, "but not much. There are also a few individuals, both domestic and foreign, who support us as well."

"How about the government? Do they give you much support?"

"The short answer to that is no, but it's a long story."

"Wait a minute. Earlier you said that the government orphanages would send you children to take care of, but now you're saying they don't give you any funding for the children. Am I understanding that correctly?"

"Yes, your comprehension is accurate. Again, there is a long story about relationships involving the government, and most foreigners have to be here a long, long time before they can begin to understand. Don't worry, they don't try to prevent me from receiving support from anyone. They just leave it up to us to manage our financial situation for ourselves."

Holly stepped over to where we were talking. "Anne and Jan," she said, "I am terribly sorry to interrupt your conversation, but my son just called and he had a surprise business trip come up, so he needs me to come and help with his child. I'm afraid we need to cut our visit short today."

Anne stood and put her hand on Holly's shoulder. "Oh, I'm sorry you need to go, but thank you so much for coming and bringing your friends and the Play-Doh to keep the children entertained."

"Darling, you know you are welcome, and I enjoy seeing the children enjoy themselves."

I turned to Anne and smiled. "Anne, thanks for being transparent with me and answering my questions. You know I work as a reporter now, so if I ask too many questions, I apologize. Please understand that it is just part of my nature. Hopefully you don't feel I'm being nosy."

"No, you're not being nosy," Anne reassured me. "I like it when people are interested in the children and what we're trying to do for them."

"Thanks, Anne. I look forward to seeing you and the kids again."

As we made our way to the door, many of the children came to see us off and to get one more hug. Their faces were so sweet and cute (and a little mischievous). I loved how they were so energetic and enthusiastic about any new game or opportunity to play. They hungered for any attention, and it wasn't difficult at all to provide that for them.

On the way back to campus, I invited Holly and Lizzy to join me for lunch sometime so I could learn more from them about Anne and the children.

Lizzy asked, "When would you like to meet? Keep in mind that I have classes and Holly has a grandchild now."

"I'm completely flexible, so whenever works the best for both of you. If you would prefer to do dinner, I could do that as well."

"Actually, dinner would work better for me," Holly said, "because my husband would be able to watch our grandbaby while I'm out."

"That makes sense. How about tomorrow?"

"That would work well for me. Lizzy, how about you?"

"Yes, that will work for me. Where do you want to go?"

"Canyon told me about a dumpling restaurant she and her husband found in town. She said it's near the river, so you get great food and a great view."

Holly looked pleased at the suggestion. "I know that restaurant well. It's a wonderful choice. I can get a driver to pick us all up at six o'clock, if that's okay with all of you."

"Yes," I said. "Let's plan on doing that, and thanks for getting us a driver."

"You're welcome. And just so you know, that restaurant has a full menu, not only dumplings, or *jiaozi,* as we call them."

8

DETERMINED TO UNDERSTAND

The weather the following day was invigorating: bright, sunny, and warm. "Hello, ladies," I said, when Holly and Lizzy met me at the south gate. "It sure is great to see you on this lovely evening! Man, there hasn't been a cloud in the sky all day long."

"Yes," Holly said wearily, "my grandson has wanted to play outside all day today, so I'm a little tired!"

"And there is another negative to such a beautiful day," Lizzy pointed out. "I catch many students staring out the window, which is where their attention is rather than in my classroom. It sounds like your grandson is already thinking like a college student, Holly."

"We do have high hopes for him but that may be a little premature, unless he gets it from his grandmother!" Holly laughed sheepishly. "Oh, I hope that didn't sound too arrogant."

"Not at all, Holly. You're a proud grandmother," I said. "That's how it sounded to me. You're tired, Lizzy is frustrated with her students' lack of attention, and I'm starved, so we are quite a group today."

"Don't worry," said Holly. "I see the driver's car coming, so we'll be at the restaurant in no time. I'm happy to hear that you're hungry, because I have a surprise for you. I've known the owner of this restaurant for years, so he said he would do a little something special for you today. I know how much you like mutton (goat) cooked on a stick over charcoal, so he will make sure he has some that's extra spicy for you tonight."

"Wow, you know everyone in this city! Thanks for making those arrangements. I can't wait to tell Canyon how good it was!" I also hoped to bring some of these good flavors home, so I asked Holly, "Do you think the owner will tell us what spices he uses? I may want to try them when I return to the States."

"He may, so I'll ask him. If I forget, though, I think I can come very close to telling you everything you will need to recreate the seasoning at home."

"That would be great, because I love to have friends or co-workers over and try to prepare some of the delicious Chinese dishes I've enjoyed."

"Speaking of your co-workers, how is your work going for you?" asked Lizzy.

"So far my boss, David, has been pleased with what I've submitted. He keeps asking me to think of the story nobody else has reported, so that is a challenge, but I don't want to talk about my work. I would rather learn more from each of you regarding Anne and the orphanage."

"What can we tell you that's worthy of a free dinner?" Lizzy asked, laughing about the tone of her own question.

"Everything! I want to know everything about the children, their health, where they came from, Anne's background, the orphanage, the apartment, the helpers, the supporters, and the funding needed to provide for so many children."

"Well, I'm not sure where to start," Holly said. "But I'll give it a try. Lizzy, please help me fill in any blanks. Anne was a senior telecommunications expert for the city, and she started volunteering at the municipal orphanage. Soon she realized that at her home she could provide better care for the children than they were receiving at the municipal orphanage, so she took some of the special needs children home with her. Because the municipal orphanage had so many children, the situation benefited everyone: the workers at the municipal orphanage would have more time, energy, and resources for the reduced number of children who were there, while Anne could provide greater individual attention to the more challenged children."

Lizzy chimed in. "That is one of the things that impresses me the most about Anne. She had a very successful career going and her own apartment, and she gave all of that up so she could provide the care the children needed. I know my job as a teacher doesn't pay nearly as much as Anne was making in her job, but I would have a hard time walking away from my income to put myself into a position where I was depending on the generosity of others."

"Yes, I see what you mean."

The driver pulled up in front of the restaurant. Holly said, "I'm sure we'll have a lot more to tell you about over dinner, but for now, look to the right of the restaurant's entrance. Do you see the charcoal for our main dish tonight?"

"Oh, I'm excited about it already. So the long rectangular tray holds the charcoal, and the meat on the sticks goes over the top of it?"

Lizzy looked pleased. "Exactly. It sounds like you're going to be able to start a restaurant when you go back to the States! But it does take some time to skewer the meat if you're cooking for many people. Did you know that people in Mongolia and Inner Mongolia really like the kind of mutton we're going to enjoy tonight?"

"No, I didn't. Aren't we a long way from Inner Mongolia?"

"You're correct again. That area of the world has lots of livestock and some beautiful grasslands, so meat is readily available."

Holly added, "It isn't only the availability of the meat that makes mutton popular in Mongolia, but also the wonderful spices they use on it."

Once we were settled comfortably at a table, I asked Lizzy and Holly what happened with the compromise I had reached with Dean Zhong about teaching approaches. Did things return to the way they were before, or had he implemented any of my suggestions? Lizzy had an encouraging report. "The compromise you reached with the dean continued, so the Foreign Language Department continues to use more modern approaches and topics than they did before."

"That's great to hear. I'm happy for the students."

A man walked up to the table, and Holly started talking to him. She seemed to know at least ninety percent of the people in the city. When they were finished conversing, Holly explained what was happening. "That man is the owner of the restaurant, and he said he's going to personally cook the meat for us. When he saw us drive up, he put some skewers of mutton over the hot coals for us, so it will be ready soon."

"That was nice of him!"

"Well, don't be surprised if he wants to take a picture of the two of you foreigners enjoying his food, so he can hang it on the wall. Hopefully you won't mind, because I told him it would be okay with you."

"Oh, too bad I didn't know that," I said. "I would have worn my shirt with the American flag on it. The students always commented when I wore it on campus."

When the server came to take our order, Holly asked, "Do you mind if I order for us? I know the best dishes here, and I also know what each of you like."

"Sounds good to me," I answered. "But please do it quickly. My schedule didn't allow me time today for lunch, so I'm famished and the food smells so good."

Holly ordered the meal for us, and spoke much faster to the server than she does with me. It remains amazing to me how Holly and Lizzy can switch so quickly from Chinese to English and then back again to Chinese.

"Okay," I said after Holly had finished ordering, "have y'all had a chance to think of any additional information you can share with me about the orphanage? I'm very interested in it, and I hope to learn more. Who knows? Maybe I can even help in some small way."

Lizzy jumped right in. "You may be interested in knowing that the orphanage has been in existence for seventeen years. I can remember going to the tenth anniversary celebration. Board members made some nice speeches, but I have three other memories from that evening. The first one was when Anne was presented with a huge photo of herself, the children, and the workers. That's the one hanging in her hallway."

"Yes, I saw it."

"The second thing I remember was the financial gift that was given to the workers. It's a custom here that people making a low salary like the workers at the orphanage receive an annual bonus equal to one month's salary. Unfortunately the orphanage was in a slow period of funding, so the workers were told they wouldn't be given their bonus. When the friends and supporters of the orphanage heard about that, everyone pitched in and raised enough money for the workers' bonuses, and they were given to them at the ceremony. All of the workers started crying when they heard the good news, and one of them—a woman—came forward and picked up the microphone. She spoke of how people coming together to help the workers made her even more determined to work hard and take good care of the children. These bold words were a big surprise, because she was extremely shy and some of the people there had probably never even heard her voice before. There weren't many dry eyes in the place then."

"What was your third takeaway?"

"Well, that would be the lives that have been changed and the love it took to change them. The workers made sure the children were dressed up and brought them to the event, where Anne insisted on sitting with them. When she took the microphone, she told some amazing stories of the lives of the children she had assisted. The children had been so young and in such desperate shape, and were completely dependent on Anne for survival. Now those same children are thriving, and some of them have been adopted. What a change—from being abandoned with a health crisis; to receiving the medical attention required, being nursed back to health, and being loved and provided for; then being adopted by a loving family, something the children had never known. The reality is that some of the children would be dead now if not for Anne."

"Wow, that is a huge transition for a child to make, and they seem to accomplish it in such a short period of time."

"Well, not all of them are lucky enough to be adopted quickly, and some are never adopted at all," Lizzy noted as she nodded toward our server, who was bringing the mutton to our table.

"Oh my gosh, that smells heavenly!" I said as the server placed the food on the table. "I didn't have lunch today, so I won't be shy. I'll take the first one."

We didn't speak much for a few minutes while we enjoyed the delicious meat, but once our conversation resumed, it went directly back to the orphans.

"So how did Anne learn so much about leading a special needs orphanage?" I asked.

"Holly, why don't you take this one while I enjoy another one of these wonderful mutton skewers," Lizzy said.

"As I said earlier, Anne was a senior telecommunications expert, so that tells you some vital information about her. Very few women her age had an opportunity to go to a university, and even fewer were given roles with some authority over men, so you can tell that she is both wise and experienced. Of course, all that is in addition to the enormously loving heart she has for the children."

"Wow, she is an impressive lady," I observed. "I imagine she has some great stories to tell about being a woman and receiving the education she did and leading her team. I would love to interview her for my stateside work!"

Lizzy offered some counsel. "Jan, allow me to give you a perspective you can relate to since we are both Americans. Before you think about interviewing Anne for an article to submit, you need to know that not everyone here is as open about their lives as people are in the States. If you ask someone a question that they don't want to answer completely or at all, it is very well accepted for them to give a vague response. If you interview Anne or any other Chinese person, you need to be able to perceive this. If you ask probing questions and get an evasive answer or two, that means they don't want to answer your question and you should move to another question, topic, or person. People can also be put off by the way we Americans ask questions. We like to drill down and get all of the details, and the Chinese take a broader view of issues. Also, Americans sometimes continue to ask questions that may lead to a negative view of the person answering the questions. You shouldn't ask questions that will paint a person into a corner. Your questions should be phrased so that the person can either answer them or have a way out that allows them to save face—that is, avoid making themselves or someone they want to protect look bad."

"Wow, that's great to know. Now I'm wondering how many people I've offended during my stays in China!"

"Jan, believe me when I tell you this," Holly began, then paused, which made me think this was going to be something especially important. "People in China can look at you and tell you are a foreigner, so they will be a little more patient with you in regard to your questions, but not too much!"

"Thanks so much for that insight. I'll definitely keep it in mind when I interact with people here."

"Ah, Jan," Holly said comfortingly, "you are a good writer, because you look for the good in a story."

"Thanks Holly. I do want to ask you something though. What was the issue you couldn't tell me about at the entrance to the orphanage?"

"About the plaques near the door of Anne's apartment, right?"

"Yes."

"There's an interesting story about them. You see, as Anne became more well-known because of all of the children she had rescued and cared for, she was asked to speak at a conference in Guangzhou. Anne is very direct and unwavering in her commitment to the children, and she didn't exactly allow for any leeway for people to save face, as Lizzy just described to you. She made it clear that she thought China needs to improve the way it educates and treats special needs orphans. So when she returned to town, government officials came in and removed the children from her because they felt her comments had cast an unfavorable light on them. Unfortunately, a couple of the children became deathly ill after they were removed from Anne, and she had a finger-pointing situation with the officials. They told Anne she didn't take good care of the children, and she told the officials that the children were fine when they left her care, so it was the people working for the officials who didn't take good care of the children. The end result was that the governing officials removed Anne's license, made it difficult for her to get children adopted, and gave her no financial aid to provide for the children even if they came from the municipal orphanage. Also, Anne now knows that the children can be removed from her again at any time."

"Oh, that's horrible!"

"I know. So those plaques near the door are to let others know that it is an approved orphanage, but the status of her license isn't as concrete as those plaques lead people to believe."

I leaned back in my chair and thought about all of this for a moment. "I never could have guessed all of that was in her past. It leads me to another question. Anne told me that she receives children from the municipal orphanage, but the government doesn't pay her to care for them. Did I understand her correctly?"

"Yes, that's correct. To my knowledge she doesn't receive any funds or compensation for helping children who come to her from the municipal orphanage."

"Okay, that's what I'm struggling with. Why would they send a child to Anne if they aren't going to help cover the expenses?"

Lizzy jumped in. "Holly, let me answer this one, and hopefully I can give Jan a clear perspective on it. You must remember that Anne started out volunteering at the municipal orphanage, so she has some wonderful relationships with the leaders and the organization. Clearly, Anne and the leaders have a mutual goal of providing the best care available for the children, so they work together for the good of the children. The financial side is secondary to the children's welfare."

"I understand, but it just seems to me like a friend wouldn't put another friend in a position that potentially would have a negative financial impact."

"Again, it is taking care of the child that is first and foremost in their minds. Also, the municipal orphanage workers are able to help Anne with some critical paperwork for the children when they are transferred to her, or even more importantly, when one of them is going to be adopted. So as you can see, they help each other and they help the children. Don't worry about Anne's relationship with the municipal orphanage. It's a good one, and it has been good for many years."

Holly noticed that the restaurant owner was walking toward our table carrying his camera. She excused herself and stood to speak with him. After a few moments, Lizzy stood up as well and motioned for me to do the same.

"He wants to take our picture to display on the wall," Lizzy explained.I proposed an idea. "How about if I put some of the skewers between my fingers and hold them sticking outward so people can see how many sticks of meat I ate. I'll look like the comic-book character Wolverine. Holly, can you relay that thought to him as I certainly don't know how to say 'Wolverine' in Chinese!" Holly and the gentleman started speaking again, and he smiled broadly and started moving his hands around in a wild manner, which led me to believe that he understood who the Wolverine character was.

"He loves your idea," Holly reported, "and he would like for you to stand near the aquarium because the lighting is better there."

"It looks like he knows who Wolverine is."

Holly nodded. "Yes, he does, and he said he is a big fan, too!"

After the owner took our picture, I asked Holly to relay a message to him. "Please thank him for cooking, and tell him how much we enjoyed our meal—especially the meat on a stick. Oh, and tell him I can't wait to come back and see our picture on the wall!"

Holly translated for me, and the owner laughed and shook our hands, then he waved good-bye and moved on to greet other guests.

"He's certainly friendly," Lizzy said.

Holly nodded her agreement. "Yes, and he's very happy about having your pictures for his wall. I can hear him telling customers now: 'Yes, our food is so good people come all the way from America for it!'"

We returned to our table and ate until we couldn't take another mouthful. At that point our conversation slowed, and so did we. The week still held more work for us, and we felt tired after the feast we had just enjoyed. Holly asked our server for containers for the remaining food so she could take some to her husband. When our waitress returned with the containers, she also had some bags filled with meat skewers. Holly said something to her, and the server pointed toward the counter, where the owner was waving at us with a huge smile on his face. We then realized that he was giving the additional food to Holly as a gift.

On our way out, I asked, "By the way, would one of you please write down the address of the orphanage in Chinese for me, so I can show it to a taxi driver? Perhaps someday I will venture there alone, but would either of you care to go tomorrow?"

Holly answered, "Yes, I do want to go to the orphanage tomorrow, and I have some card games for the children. I also have a yoyo, so we may all need to wear a helmet! Jan, I have a business card I can give you that has the address in both English and Chinese."

"Thanks Holly, that would be great! Lizzy, are you in?"

"Sure, it will make my day to see all of those smiling faces."

"Yeah, I know what you mean, they have grown on me. I can see their cute, sweet, mischievous faces in my mind!"

9

WHERE IS SHE?

As we approached the orphanage, I asked Lizzy and Holly to let me lead the way because I wanted to make sure I could find the right building, floor, and apartment. They looked at each other and smiled, remembering all of the other times I had asked to lead the way, speak to the taxi driver, or order food. It seemed like every time I needed one of them to rescue me from my language failures, we could always have a good laugh about it. It's a true gift to have friends so close that they can laugh at your fumbles with kindness and good humor. While spending time in China, I have had many occasions to laugh at myself.

As we walked past the playground located in an open area between the apartment buildings, Lizzy said, "It's a nice day; perhaps we can bring the children outside to play."

"I was just thinking the same thing!" Holly said. "I love to watch them run and play, and I feel so sorry for them because they don't get to do that very often since there aren't enough adults at the orphanage to take them outside."

I was surprised. "Holly, are you kidding me? They don't get to come outside and play every day?"

"No, I'm sorry to tell you that they don't. Not only are there times when there aren't enough adults to accompany them, sometimes Anne feels that certain people who want to know more about her orphanage may be hiding and watching the children as they play. They do this in an attempt to know exactly how many children are there."

"Wow, where I grew up, we went outside to play every day unless the weather was bad."

Lizzy said, "Then you'll truly appreciate the children's excitement when it is announced that we'll take them outside. You won't understand what Anne says, but you'll see the children jumping up and down, and you'll hear them screaming while they scramble to get their shoes on."

"I don't blame them. I think all children should have the opportunity to play outside. I may be a little bit of a tomboy, and I did grow up in homes with several other children, but it just seems natural to me." I noticed a ramp at the end of the stairs going into the building and asked if it was for the children in wheelchairs.

Holly nodded. "Yes, it's for anyone in a wheelchair, and people making deliveries use it as well."

"Okay, I know I can lead us to the elevator, select the correct floor, and find the right apartment, so I think I'll pass this test! I imagine some days you can get off on the correct floor and use your sense of hearing to find the orphanage itself."

"I think you're right about that!"

"Do you know how other people in the building feel about the noise?"

"In my opinion," Holly answered, "because the neighbors have all seen the plaques around the front door, they know that the government has approved the special needs orphanage being there. So there isn't much they can do about it if they have a problem. Also, I believe that the residents understand the situation, so they are forgiving of some of the noise, and I'm sure they enjoy seeing all of the smiling faces too."

"If I may add a little something to that," Lizzy said, "I've watched the parents and children interact with the orphans on the playground. The children seem to play well together, and many times the parents encourage their children to interact with our little buddies. When we bring the children outside to play, we normally bring balls, hula hoops, or bubbles to blow, and they are very good about sharing their toys with other children on the playground. I guess they're used to sharing, since they are constantly surrounded by other children."

We stepped off the elevator and rounded the corner. "Well, here we are. I found it! Who would like the honor of ringing the doorbell and entering first?"

"Jan, you are the youngest, so you go first. As you enter, you can protect Holly and me from the stampede of children!"

"Oh, I see, this is one of those let-the-newest-person-go-first situations!" I rang the bell, and we all laughed because we could hear the children shouting and rushing toward the door. As the door opened, it was a blessing to see so many smiling children, all happy to see us. Like the other times, they excitedly held their arms up in anticipation, so we put our things down and picked up as many children as we could. Anne and one of the workers sat on a sofa folding towels, and one little girl, about three years old, was helping them as best she could.

"Hello Anne," I said. "How are you and the children today? Holly, Lizzy, and I are impressed with the wonderful greeting we receive whenever we come here."

"We're doing well, and it's nice to see you today. Yes, the children enjoy seeing who's behind the door when the doorbell rings. They are always hopeful it is someone who will play with them."

I sat on the other end of the sofa, and the child I was holding ran away to play with some of the other children. I noticed a children's book on the arm of the sofa, so I opened it and had a look. As I began thumbing through the pages, one of the little girls crawled up onto the sofa and into my lap. She was a tiny little girl, and she was precious. She would turn the pages for me and point to things in the pictures. She spoke softly while she entertained herself, and I noticed something I had never seen before. Her fingernails were blue. Not blue from nail polish, but blue under her fingernails. I looked more closely at my new friend, and I could see that her lips were blue as well, and I could hear that her breathing was raspy.

"Anne, can you tell me what she's saying as she points at the pictures? The book is in English, so I know she doesn't understand it."

"She's telling you what she sees."

"Would you like me to teach her the English words for the items she likes in the pictures?"

"Sure, you can teach all of the children if you'd like to!"

"Wow, that would be a big task. Maybe someday I'll be up to the challenge. What is this darling little girl's name? She has such beautiful, shiny hair."

"Her name is Xiao Ting."

"Well Xiao Ting, it is nice to meet you!"

She looked up at me when I said her name, and I will never forget her beautiful eyes. They communicated so many things all at one time. It was as if I was looking into her soul and she was saying, *help me, please help me.* I sensed that she was a very intelligent girl—playful, loving, and friendly. Also I could see in her eyes that she was tired and weak.

"Anne, may I ask what is medically wrong with Xiao Ting?"

"She has a hole in her heart."

"Is it bad?"

"Yes. When she feels weak and tired, she is afraid to play with the other children. When she feels well, she's in the middle of everything that's going on, and she tries to boss the other children around even though she's younger than they are."

"Is it the hole in her heart that causes her fingers and lips to be blue?"

"Yes," Anne said. "Without the proper amount of oxygen going through her body, her lips and fingers turn blue. The doctors say she needs an operation soon."

"I don't want to seem rude, but why just *soon*? Why not immediately?"

"The doctors feel that she needs to grow and become stronger, and I need money for the surgery and personnel to help her during her stay in the hospital."

"Okay, I understand her needing to be a little stronger and larger, but what do you mean by having personnel to stay with her at the hospital?"

"The hospitals in China and the US don't work the same way. In China, the hospital only provides beds, performs medical procedures, and prescribes medication as needed. If a patient is in her room and needs to go to the X-ray laboratory, then she will need to have a family member or a friend push her in a wheelchair to the laboratory. The same holds true for meals. For most patients, the hospital doesn't provide any meals, so the patient needs a friend or family member to bring in meals."

"I've never heard of that approach, but I guess it does leave the medical team to focus on the medical issues and not transportation and meals. So will you have the money ready for her surgery when she has grown enough?"

Anne shook her head. "No, our finances are a little behind currently. There is a church in Hong Kong that has supported us for years, but their contributions have dropped to less than what they pledged."

"How much would you estimate the cost of an operation like the one Xiao Ting needs?"

"The doctors say it will cost around $8,800 in US dollars. I am fortunate because some of the doctors know me and know that I am helping the children, so they may give me a reduced price."

"Will insurance cover any of the medical expenses for Xiao Ting?"

"She is an orphan, so she doesn't have any insurance."

"How long will the hospital and doctors give you to pay the bill?"

"This is another way the hospitals in China differ from those in the States. In China, you must pay for the medical procedure before the operation. Since I have brought so many children to the number two hospital for medical attention, sometimes the doctors won't make me pay the entire medical bill prior to the operation. One doctor who performs eye operations makes me pay only eighty percent up front, and then he will usually allow me to have a couple of months to pay the remaining twenty percent. I wish all of the doctors were that kind, but only a few of them will do that. The doctors who give me a little extra time know I'm helping orphans, so they are willing to help me out a little with the bills."

I sat there stunned. I couldn't imagine how many times Anne must have had to struggle to get enough cash to pay for a medical procedure for one of the children. As I tried to process the information, I realized that if a hospital wanted to be profitable, this was an attractive business model. Not having a collections department would mean great savings, not to mention having no delinquent payments. I also realized that I was coming up with some new topics for my reporting job, so I was thankful I had asked those questions.

"Thanks for taking the time to talk with me, Anne. Holly, Lizzy, and I discussed taking the children outside to play today. Would that be agreeable to you?"

"Yes, the children love going outside to play, and this looks like a nice day. We should have a couple of additional helpers with the children because some of the students will be here soon. Maybe we could take them across the street to the park, which would give them a little more room than the playground between the buildings."

"That sounds good to me. I'll let Lizzy and Holly know. This will be my first time going outside to play with the children. Will Xiao Ting be able to go with us?"

"Yes, she can go, but we will take her to the park in a stroller. All of that walking would make her tired and she would start wheezing, and then she wouldn't feel like playing."

"Oh, well we certainly want her to feel like playing, so I'll push her stroller myself, if that's okay."

"Sure, that will be fine, and I know Xiao Ting will enjoy having more attention from you. Watch what happens when I tell the children to get ready to go to the park. They'll be in a mad rush to get their shoes on."

When the students arrived to help, Anne said something to the children, and they certainly did go crazy. One threw a deck of cards into the air, a couple of boys raced to the cabinet by the door and started putting on their shoes, and the workers picked up some of the children who couldn't walk and put them in wheelchairs or strollers. It was touching to see two of the older girls volunteering to push the children in strollers. Some of the children grabbed hula hoops, one had a soccer ball, and a girl had some badminton rackets and a birdie. The energy level was intense. You could tell that the children putting on their shoes were doing it as quickly as they possibly could. The workers were tucking some bags under the seats of the strollers and in the pockets of the wheelchairs. There was a girl with cerebral palsy who was nonverbal and normally only lay on a bed, so I was surprised to see one of the workers and Anne help her into a wheelchair. Some of the boys were jumping up and down and turning in circles. Seeing the joy on their faces was priceless.

When Anne said all of the children were ready to go to the elevator, there was a crazy rush to the door until the apartment looked empty. As we arrived at the elevators, the children had already started playing with their hula hoops and the soccer ball. The elevator door opened, and several children raced in. They needed to have some adults with them, so Lizzy held the door and told a couple of the children to move out of the way so adults could get on the elevator. When the second elevator's doors opened, the process repeated itself, and the children clapped.

When the elevators arrived on the ground floor, we exited and walked down the ramp. One of the workers was telling the children to line up, but the line wasn't very straight. Anne's group was the last to arrive. She motioned for the workers to start walking toward the gated entrance of the apartment complex. Some of the children skipped on their own, some walked holding an adult's hand, and some were being pushed in their wheelchairs or strollers. Xiao Ting looked around in amazement as if this were the first trip she had ever taken outside. Then her interest shifted to the items in the pocket of her stroller. Apparently her favorite thing was the bottle of soapy water and the wand that would be inside for blowing bubbles.

We made it through the gate leading to the street. The security guard had a funny look on his face when everyone—children and adults with toys in hand—came traipsing through the gate he had raised for us. I became a little nervous about our next challenge: crossing a very busy street to reach the park. One of the workers was holding a couple of the children's hands, and hollering at others who looked like they were about to dart into the street. When Anne said go, we all went, but at different speeds. The curb on the other side of the street slowed down the wheelchairs and strollers, and the group started to become scattered as some of the children ran ahead. A motorcycle whizzed past us on the street before we all were finished crossing.

Finally we were all safely across the street, and it was a huge relief for me and the other adults. We were able to put some of the children down because they could walk the rest of the way. The children knew exactly where to cut through a hole in the bushes and go into the park. Once we cleared the bushes, I was extremely impressed with what I saw.

Directly ahead of us were several ping-pong tables, some of which were being used, as well as clusters of outdoor exercise equipment and some monkey bars. The beautiful park was full of trees and flowers, and there was a covered area where several older people were playing music, singing, and dancing.

Xiao Ting started jerking in the stroller like she was riding a bucking bronco, so I knew she was ready to go. The children went to an open area where some started playing soccer and badminton, and others used chalk to draw pictures on the pavement. I lifted Xiao Ting from the stroller, and she found a comfortable spot and started blowing bubbles and watching with fascination as they floated away. Several children joined her with their own bottles of bubble solution, and some others came over to catch or pop the bubbles.

Flowing through the park was a creek, and some of the boys couldn't resist throwing rocks into the water. The adults saw how dangerous it was for the boys to be so close to the water's edge, so a couple of us stayed there with the boys. As I was listening to the older people singing and watching the children play, I noticed that there was a constant stream of people walking or riding their bikes through the park. Clearly the park was strategically placed, and was both needed and appreciated.

To my surprise, one of the little girls who had always appeared to be very shy came to me without her crutches and took my hand. She pointed to the monkey bars, and I walked with her. She climbed up and hung upside down, giggling as her hair covered her face. A couple of her buddies came and joined her on the monkey bars, and I remembered that I had my camera in my pocket. I asked Anne if it was okay if I took their picture.

"Sure," Anne replied. "The girls like to have their picture taken, and I'm very happy to see that you have a camera because I would like to get a group picture taken near the creek."

"Okay, just let me know when you want to bring everyone together for that picture."

I gestured to the three girls on the monkey bars that I was going to take their pictures. Excitedly, they came together, and the shy girl made a peace sign. For the remainder of the pictures, all of them made peace signs, even if they were hanging upside down and their hair covered their faces.

I heard Anne calling out to the children and pointing to an area near the creek, and the girls on the monkey bars climbed down and started making their way to where she had pointed. The shy girl grabbed my hand—which I felt was a huge honor—and off we went. When we came to her crutches, she picked them up and began using them, so she no longer needed to hold my hand.

The children, workers, and volunteers came together in the designated area, and I began taking pictures. Soon I saw Anne jump like she had been stung by a hornet, and she started to speak quickly to the others. A couple of the workers ran away from the group, shouting. Something was wrong, but I wasn't sure what. I asked Holly what was going on.

She explained quickly, "When we came together for the pictures, Anne wanted to make sure all of the children were there and she realized that a little girl named Lily is missing, so now everyone needs to look for her. Lily is developmentally challenged, and we have no idea of where she may be or what might have happened to her."

I was startled and worried. "Oh my goodness, how can I help?"

"Well, you can run faster than me, so I will stay here with the children as everyone else scours the park. If you go in the direction of the big gazebo where the people were singing, that will complete our search grid. Everyone will rendezvous back here. Hurry!"

I began running toward the gazebo, my mind racing with thoughts about where Lily could be—or even worse, what could have happened to her. Because I had asked Anne if we could take the children outside, I felt responsible for Lily. If anything happened to her, I didn't know what I would do. I circled the gazebo but didn't see her. I made a couple of larger circles around the gazebo to no avail, then decided I should return to the group in hopes of hearing good news.

"Holly, did anyone find Lily?" I asked when I rejoined my friend.

"No. Everyone who searched the park is back from their assigned areas. We're all worried silly."

"What will we do next?"

"Anne has gone back to the apartment with a couple of the older children, and she said for the rest of us to come along when we regroup."

One of the workers shouted something to the children, and they started gathering into something that vaguely resembled a line. Again, some of the small children were carried by adults and others were in strollers and wheelchairs. Some of the older children were carrying the toys they had brought to the park. With Anne back at the apartment, I was concerned about everyone crossing the street safely. Lizzy held out her arm to stop the children from going into the street too soon, and a large truck drove by so quickly that everyone's hair blew and our shirts fluttered in the wind. Lizzy motioned for everyone to cross the street after the truck passed. Thankfully the volume of traffic had diminished since our initial crossing, and we were able to regroup by the gate without incident.

As we approached the ramp at the apartment building, Anne came bursting outside and delivered some great news. Lily was fine! She was in the apartment. Apparently she had slipped away unnoticed when we walked past the courtyard playground. One of the neighbors recognized her and knew where she lived, so she returned Lily to the apartment. A worker who had stayed behind to work on the laundry took care of her until Anne returned. Anne told us that Lily loved to jump on the trampoline in the courtyard playground, and that is where the neighbor found her.

Finally we could all breathe a sigh of relief. Lizzy, Holly, and I smiled at each other and began walking the children into the apartment building. What a range of emotions we had experienced in the last half hour!

As it worked out, Xiao Ting and I were the last ones to get on the elevator. Once the doors closed and we felt the elevator move, she gave me a very loving smile as if to say thank you for taking her outside to play. She reached up with both of her arms, so I knew she wanted to be held. I took her from the stroller and held her. By the time we got to the apartment door, she was almost asleep.

There in the apartment was Lily, playing with some balloons Lizzy had brought. Lizzy's cheeks were bright red from blowing them up. In a sign of surrender, she gave one of the workers the small bag of balloons to distribute to the children. A couple of the older boys could blow them up, but they needed instructions on how to tie them.

By this time Xiao Ting was sound asleep with her head on my shoulder, and I made my way over to Anne. "Is it normal for her to fall asleep while being held by someone?"

"Yes," Anne replied. "She is weak from the condition in her heart, so playing outside made her very tired. I think all of the children will sleep well tonight!"

"That's good news for you and the night staff, I'm sure."

"Oh, there is no night staff! I'm here alone with the children from bedtime until they get up in the morning. I take care of the sick ones, give medicine, and take kids to the bathroom all night long."

"When do you sleep?"

"I sleep when I can, but I probably average around three hours a night. That's all I've had for years, so that is all I need."

"You are an amazing woman, Anne. And I give you a lot of credit for leaving a successful career to have all of these children living in your apartment with you. I don't think I could do what you do daily."

"Well, I love the children, so I want to provide a loving home for them, and this is the best I can do."

"The children certainly are fortunate to have such a loving person taking care of them," I said. "Speaking of taking care of the children, I'm so sorry Lily got lost today. I feel as if it was my fault because I asked you about taking them outside to play."

"Don't worry yourself about Lily," Anne said in a comforting tone. "It wasn't your fault, nor was it my fault. We adults didn't pay enough attention, and there are so many children to watch, so we all share collectively in any blame. I knew she couldn't have gone far, since our apartment complex is fully enclosed. I had a feeling we would have found her quickly if she was still in the park, so I raced back with a couple of the older children to help in the search if we needed to continue looking."

"You are more than kind for not being upset about this. I can assure you that if I help with an outing again, I'll count how many children we have when we leave, and I'll count them as we play, and again when we return."

"You sound like a school teacher now!"

Holly walked over to where Anne and I were talking. "Jan, it's getting late," she said, "and Holly and I need to start heading back to the campus."

"Let me put Xiao Ting in her bed, and I'll be right with you." I turned to Anne and asked, "Which crib would you like me to place Xiao Ting in?"

"She likes to be in the one beside the bunk beds in the far corner from the door."

As I walked into the large back bedroom, I paid more attention to the room than I had before. There were several wooden cribs that looked well-made and heavy, but they definitely showed signs of wear and tear. They were significantly larger than cribs in the States, and I recalled seeing multiple children in them before. The sheets in all of the cribs looked worn but not dirty. I couldn't imagine the expense of providing for so many children. As I bent over to remove Xiao Ting from my shoulder and place her in the crib, I noticed she still had her bottle of bubbles in her hand. This brought back memories for me from when I lived in foster homes. Anything I could call my own was very special.

As we headed back down to the lobby, the elevator seemed so much roomier than when we had the children, strollers, and toys with us. I was once again full of questions, so I proposed that we have coffee. Lizzy suggested a Starbucks near People's Square.

I turned to Holly. "Would your schedule allow you to hang out at Starbucks for a little while?"

"Sure," she said. "Just let me call my husband and let him know I will be a little later than I told him. He's a worrier, if I'm not home when I tell him I'll be there, but you would think after so many years of marriage he would know that sometimes my plans change."

10

THE CHILDREN

We waved down a taxi on the same street we had previously crossed with the children, and Holly sat in front so she could tell the driver where to go. The driver chuckled when Holly told him that we wanted to go to Starbucks. I guess he thought that was pretty typical for foreigners. He may have been a little surprised, however, to hear Holly speaking English so fluently with us. Holly said she would pay for the taxi, so I offered to pay for the drinks. Lizzy said that sounded great to her, and we all laughed.

The Starbucks smelled wonderful as we entered. Lizzy found us a table, and Holly and I ordered the drinks and carried them to the table. Once we were settled, I broke the ice. "Okay, I feel horrible about not knowing how many children we left the apartment with and for letting Lily wander away from us."

Holly put her hand on my arm reassuringly. "Please don't feel badly about it. The workers, Anne, and I have all seen the chaos before, so we should have known better ourselves. Don't keep beating yourself up about it."

I took a deep breath. "Okay, I'll try. Maybe if I change the subject, that will help get my mind off of it. So can either of you tell me about the little boy who could climb the monkey bars so well? I even saw him climbing a tree until Anne told him to come down. He has scars on his face. What is his story?"

Lizzy explained. "Yeah, his name is Meng He, and we don't know how he got the burn scars on his face. He was abandoned at the hospital, so the hospital called Anne. We believe that his parents knew they could not afford the medical attention he needed, so they left him at the hospital in hopes that he would receive care. When Anne first received Meng He, the medical team had to remove scarred skin from around his eye because he couldn't see out of it."

"Oh my gosh, that must have been horrible for the little guy! I'm sure he had to endure a lot of pain when all that happened, but he seems to have adjusted well. Would you agree?"

"Yes, I think so," Lizzy said. "But there are a couple of additional things you should know about Meng He. The schools didn't want to allow him to attend because they were afraid that the children would pick on him so much that it would hurt his feelings and lead to some emotional problems. Also, he doesn't like to have his picture taken. Did you notice that today in the park?"

"Now that I think of it, Lizzy, I did notice that he stood behind someone when we were taking pictures, and when Anne made him come out from behind them, he faced away from the camera. So what is the status of his enrollment in school?"

"This is one thing that we all appreciate about Anne. She fought the school and whoever was a decision maker on this, and she called in some favors from people she knew, and finally Meng He was allowed to enter school. He's doing very well. He has the second highest math grades in his class!"

"Well good for him! I knew I liked him right away. He seemed so happy running around and climbing. I noticed when I saw you playing with him, Lizzy, that he can even climb people."

"Yeah, Meng He is a good climber, and he brings a high level of energy into the room when he enters."

"There is another boy almost the same size as Meng He, and they seem to play together almost all the time. He has a darling face, but you can tell there is a little mischief in him. What is that boy's story?"

"Let me tell his story, Lizzy," Holly said, "and you can enjoy your latte." Holly turned to me and tapped her finger on her upper lip. "His name is Jing Jing, and you have to look very closely at his face to see it, but he had a cleft palate."

"Isn't a cleft palate easy to repair?" I asked. "Why is he in a special needs orphanage?"

"The restoration of a cleft palate requires multiple operations, so as with Meng He, maybe his parents knew they couldn't afford to provide the care he needed, so perhaps they abandoned him in hopes of providing for his needs that way."

"Man, it is so sad that families can't provide surgeries for children they obviously love. How ironic that the only way they can care for them is by giving them up. Sad. Just tragic."

"Here is some good news for you about Jing Jing. Anne has legally adopted him, so he knows his future is with his Mama. Have you noticed how all of the children call Anne 'Mama'?"

"Yes, I have noticed the children calling her Mama, and I think that is so heartwarming. It must make Anne feel wonderful. It probably gives her an emotional lift on her tough days! The next child I want to ask about is a boy much older and larger than the other children. I can tell he had a cleft palate too. I noticed that he doesn't play with the other children very much, but he did play with some older children in the park."

Lizzy said, "Holly, you'd better try to answer this question too, because I'm not sure I could do justice to all of the events in his life and the laws pertaining to his situation."

"Laws?"

"Yes, laws," Holly began. "His name is Paul, and he has a tragic story. When he was born, he did indeed have a cleft palate, and you can still see the scars above his lip. He is from another province and he was abandoned by his parents, so a very old couple took him in. However, they soon realized that Paul's needs were much too challenging for them, so they gave him to a younger couple. This younger couple tried to provide for Paul, but his condition was too severe even for them, so they gave him to an orphanage in their province. If you recall, we told you that Anne has a reputation for helping children, especially since she was asked to speak at that conference, so somehow the orphanage contacted Anne and she came to get him. Not long ago, Paul had his third operation for his cleft palate. I think the first one closed his lip, the second closed his gums, and the third one closed the canyon in the roof of his mouth. Interestingly, the first thing he said after the last surgery was that he could hear much better."

I was surprised. "I wouldn't have thought of that helping his hearing, but once you think about the proximity of the roof of his mouth and his inner ear, that makes sense. What grade is he in?"

Lizzy said, "See, this is why I wanted Holly to answer your question, because this is hard for Americans to comprehend."

"What is it, Holly?"

"Well, when Paul was born, his parents abandoned him and they never registered him. Maybe they were thinking that this way they could have another baby and hopefully it would be healthy, but I'm only guessing. Anyway, the older couple never registered him, nor did the younger couple or the orphanage."

"Okay, so nobody registered him. What does that mean for Paul?"

"Oh, this is a big deal in China! In our country everyone needs to be registered. The registration card is called a Hukou, which is very similar to your Social Security card. In China if you don't have a Hukou, you can't go to school or get any job."

"But he does attend school, so how can he do that if he isn't registered?"

"You know that Anne won't back down from a fight for any of the children. Well, Paul is a great example of that. Initially, he wasn't allowed to go to school, but Anne continued to work on getting him enrolled, and finally the school system allowed him to attend. I'm sure Anne had to exhaust all of her *Guanxi*, or relationships, to get Paul enrolled. This is one situation in which her wonderful relationship with the municipal orphanage may have helped. Actually, we don't know what happened or how it happened, but we know we like the result, so we don't need to know anything else. Paul is in school, and we got to witness Anne's determination to get him enrolled. He had been getting into a little bit of trouble at school, but after his last surgery, his grades have improved, so maybe his hearing was more of an issue than we knew."

"Anne has certainly fought a lot of battles for her children! I want to always be on her good side, because it sounds like she will take on anyone who isn't giving the children the opportunities they need."

"You are right about that," said Lizzy.

"Okay, so what about Paul's future, since he is without a Hukou?"

Lizzy turned to Holly. "Man, I am thankful you are here to answer these questions," she said.

Holly took a sip of coffee and thought for a moment. "You need to understand a couple of issues about the challenges facing Paul. I'm told there is a law that at the age of fourteen a child is technically no longer allowed to remain in an orphanage."

"Are you kidding me? You can't put a fourteen-year-old out on the street!"

"Now hold on and let me finish," Holly said. "I've never seen this law in writing, and I don't even know if it's enforced strictly or not, but that's what I've been told."

"So what kinds of options would he have? What kind of job could he get at the age of fourteen? Where can he go to school if Anne isn't there to fight for his enrollment?"

Lizzy laughed. "Holly, I knew this would get Jan's blood boiling."

Holly continued, "Paul will continue to struggle with his education after he leaves his current school because he doesn't have his

Hukou. Schools aren't allowed to accept students that aren't legally registered. Likewise, employment will be a challenge because he technically doesn't exist."

Lizzy was right. My blood was boiling. "Paul is a young guy now," I said. "When he's twenty-five, can he apply for his Hukou then?"

"If you don't have your Hukou from birth," Holly insisted, "it is virtually impossible to get one. This will be a problem for him all of his life, and it will probably haunt him whenever he tries to enroll in school, take a job, or even get a loan."

"Oh my gosh, I feel so sorry for him! What do you think his future holds?"

"I really don't know. I just know that the road through his future will have many challenges."

"Okay, here's a crazy thought: what if he were adopted by a family in a country where he doesn't need a Hukou?"

"Without his Hukou, he can't even be registered to be adopted."

"Man, I will struggle getting my head around this Hukou thing. I guess it's like how we want everyone to have a Social Security number to get a job in the States. That way everyone knows that a person is legally in the country and paying taxes correctly."

Lizzy nodded. "You're right, Jan. That's the closest thing we have in the States."

There was another child I was curious about. "You know the little girl who seems to be very shy, and she uses crutches that kind of encircle her arm? I'm wondering about her, too."

"Yes, I know which girl you mean," Lizzy said. "I can handle this one, Holly. Her name is Tammie, and she is a wonderful example of the great relationship Anne has with the municipal orphanage. The leader of the municipal orphanage asked Anne to help her with Tammie, because Tammie needed surgery on both of her clubfeet. They knew that Tammie's recovery would be better with Anne because she would receive more attention; and then there's her other condition."

"What other condition?"

"Tammie has spina bifida, but she had some complications with her diagnosis. She also has tethered spine syndrome, so messages don't travel up and down her spine as needed. Therefore, she has to wear a diaper, and the schools won't allow anyone wearing a diaper to attend."

"That's terrible! Was Anne able to use her *Guanxi* to get Tammie enrolled?"

"Unfortunately, it didn't work out in Anne's favor this time. Perhaps you have noticed another boy and girl who are active but don't walk without assistance. The boy scoots himself around quickly on the floor, and he had a wheelchair for today's excursion outside. The girl has the cutest dimples, and she uses crutches just like Tammie's, but she usually walks on her knees. Well, they also have spina bifida with tethered spine syndrome, wear diapers, and can't go to school. Ming Ming is the boy's name, and he gets some really bad sores on his lower body from constantly moving around on the floor. Likewise, the little girl with the dimples, Qing Qing, has a deep wound on the heel of one of her feet due to her condition. She can actually walk without the crutches, but Anne doesn't want her to walk, because if she does her wound won't heal."

"That is so sad for the children, and it sounds like Anne will continually have medical bills to pay for them. Did I hear Qing Qing counting to twenty in Spanish for you today, Holly?"

"Yes, you did. A volunteer named Brenda taught a few of the children to do that."

"So it sounds like Qing Qing could do well in school, except she isn't allowed to attend."

"Yes, that's correct. She's a clever and charming girl, but unfortunately she can't be enrolled in school."

"Okay, I understand that, but what about other options? What about homeschooling or a private tutor? There has to be something that can be done for children in such circumstances."

Lizzy shook her head no. "As Holly can tell you, homeschooling doesn't really happen here like it does in the States, but I understand your logic. Also, Anne doesn't have the resources to pay for a private tutor for the children. In fact, she already struggles to provide for their medical needs, keep them in school, pay the workers' salaries, and keep the children fed. She does her best to save money where she can, and her brother-in-law volunteers daily to do all of their cooking and some small repair jobs. This is a tremendous gesture on his part, because he and his wife provide for a special needs child of their own at home."

"That really is a huge sacrifice. I wish I could help in some way. How much would it cost to have a private tutor come and help children like Ming Ming and Qing Qing?"

"It would depend on the education and experience level of the tutor and how often they visited. I would think you could get someone with previous teaching experience for about sixteen dollars an hour."

"I could handle that amount myself, and it would be wonderful for the children! I should be able to afford it because I think my financial future is about to get a little brighter. I recently heard from David, my boss, and he said there has been significant progress with the development of a position for which he is grooming me, so he wants me back in the States before the end of next week. He indicated that my salary will increase greatly with my new position, and I want to use some of it to help Anne and the children."

"Jan, congratulations to you on your new position," Holly said, smiling broadly. "But we will miss you so much here!"

"Well, I have a feeling that I may do some traveling with this new role, so any opportunities I have to return will be accepted. Do you think if I asked Anne for a list of her needs and desires for the children she would be open to telling me? I have a couple of other thoughts about how I can help all of them."

Lizzy echoed Holly. "First of all, let me also congratulate you on your new position and wish you the best of luck. I'm sorry to hear that you're leaving, but I'm thrilled to hear of your advancement with your career, and we do hope you'll be able to return often. And yes, I'm sure Holly would agree that Anne would tell you what they need and what she envisions them having."

"Wonderful, because I plan to get my friends at work to help support Anne and the children. I think our first challenge will be to raise the funds required to get Xiao Ting's operation done. Do you know of anything more pressing than her operation?"

"No, I don't think we do," Holly answered, "but I'm sure Anne will be able to give you quite a list."

"Since I'm leaving soon, I need to complete some work assignments. I also plan to spend significantly more time with Anne and the children before I leave. In fact, I think I will return tomorrow afternoon. Would either of you care to join me?"

"I have previous plans," Lizzy said, "and it sounds like you will have lots to discuss with Anne, so I wouldn't want to get in your way."

"How about you, Holly, would you like to return with me?"

"Indeed I would, but I'm keeping my grandbaby all day tomorrow, so I'm afraid it will be out of the question for me."

"Okay, well, we will have to plan more time together before I leave, and I want you both to know how much I appreciate your taking so much time with me during this trip. Thank you for opening my eyes to Anne's world."

11

THE LIST

I called ahead to make sure Anne would have some time to spend with me, and I told her that I would be returning to the States soon. She was very agreeable about meeting with me and I planned to bring my camera, tape recorder, and notepad.

When I rang the doorbell, I could hear the children coming to the door, one of my favorite experiences of visiting the orphanage. When the door opened, there were so many children with smiling faces, happy to see me. The girls were so cute this time because they all had brightly colored ribbons in their hair.

As I greeted Anne, I picked up one of the little girls. "I love the ribbons in the girls' hair, Anne. Did you do that all by yourself?"

"Yes, I did it by myself, and thank you for noticing. The girls feel very playful today with their new ribbons, but some of the boys are already trying to untie them."

"Maybe the boys are jealous about the attention the girls are getting."

"No, I think they are just being boys!" We both had a good laugh as we watched their mischief.

"Thank you for agreeing to let me ask you more questions today," I said. "It seems like that's all I do when we're together."

"No problem," Anne said. "I'm thankful for anyone who is interested in the children. How about if we go to my office so it will be quieter?"

"Oh, I didn't know you had an office, so you lead the way."

"Maybe I need to show you more of the apartment, so you will have a better understanding of our facility and how we operate."

"That sounds like a good idea." We walked through the apartment to a hallway, where I saw three doors I had never noticed before. Anne opened the door on the left, and I was amazed by what was inside. The room may have been called her office, but it was originally designed as a bedroom; now it was as much a storage area as an office. Anne cleared a path to her desk, on which I saw computer equipment, notebooks, and many file folders. Around the perimeter of the room were shelves full of books, additional desks, and locked medical cabinets. The cabinets had wooden doors on the bottom and locked glass doors on top, so you could see the medicines, gauze, tape, and ointments inside them. The room was also filled with stuffed animals, books, and boxes of various shapes and sizes. There were also many huge containers of individually-wrapped snacks for the children. The ceiling was at least sixteen feet high, and the room was almost at capacity.

"Here, you take this chair, and I'll get another one," Anne said. She scooted the chair from in front of the desk toward me, and she moved some boxes and retrieved another chair for herself. "So, what did you want to discuss today?"

"First of all, I want to thank you for the love, patience, and kindness you give to the children. When I hear all of them calling you Mama, it truly touches my soul because I never knew my mother. I also want to thank you for allowing me to take pictures of the children and your home, and for permitting me to record my time here. I'll only show these pictures to my friends. I won't post anything on the internet, nor will I use the children's names."

"You're welcome, Jan. When Holly and Lizzy told me you were coming here, I thought you would have one of two reactions. Either you would be very engaged with the children, or the experience would bring back bad memories which would stop you from having anything to do with them."

"I knew I would enjoy my time with you and the children as soon as I saw all of the smiling faces greeting us at the door, and I could see how much the children wanted us to hold them and play with them. There is no other place on the planet where I am greeted like that!" I pulled out my notepad and pen. "As I told you on the phone, I don't have much time left in your city so I want to learn as much as I can about you, the children, your needs, and how I can serve all of you after I get home."

"Okay," Anne said, "let's get started, and I'll try to answer you as best as I can."

"Thanks. Let's start with Xiao Ting because I have truly bonded with her. If I remember correctly, you said it would cost about $8,800 US dollars for her surgery. Is that correct?"

"Yes, your memory is very good."

"Thanks. I wrote the details down as soon as I could because this is important to me. I wanted to talk to you about raising support for Xiao Ting's operation when I return home. I believe I can get my friends at work to contribute until we have enough. Does that sound good to you?"

Anne smiled broadly. "Oh, I can't begin to tell you how happy that makes me, because last night Xiao Ting fainted. She was playing with the children in the big room and just collapsed. She woke up immediately, and I took her to the hospital where she saw her heart doctor. He examined her and determined that her condition had worsened so much he can no longer wait for her growth. She needs the surgery now. In fact, the doctor wanted me to leave her in the hospital so she could be on oxygen and so they could do more testing."

"Oh no! I'm so sorry to hear that! I did look for her when we walked through the big room and when I didn't see her, I thought she might be in the bedroom. I promise you that when I return home, raising support for her operation will be one of my highest priorities! I should be able to wire the money to you soon after I return."

"Thank you so much. I didn't know where I was going to get the money, so I am very thankful for your generous offer."

"It is an honor for me to help, and I think my friends in the States will be happy to get involved as well. Now, please tell me about your needs for this apartment."

"You are thinking big, aren't you? Well, the children need work done to their bathroom, because only one of the three sinks works. Also, when we give the children a bath, we use a plastic children's swimming pool and fill it with hot water heated in the kitchen. I would like to have a shower for them and a high-efficiency water heater. There is a clothes washer in the children's bathroom, but it's very old and doesn't clean their clothes very well. Oh, and the toilet seat is broken, so a new toilet seat would be very nice to have."

"Okay, this is a good start. What else would enhance the children's lives?"

"As you can see, someone donated some very strong bunk beds for the back bedroom. This was because I organized the Special Olympics in our city. They also gave a set of bunk beds for the big room for the older boys."

"Yes, I have noticed those bunk beds, and the wood looks shiny and strong. So you organized a Special Olympics here?"

"Yes, one of the local schools let us use their facility, and the event has grown larger and larger each year. Last year we had over a hundred participants and over three hundred volunteers!"

"Wow, that's amazing, and supported so well!"

"We've been pleased with the growth. I have a DVD of the event I can show you, and the children love to watch it because some of them did a dance routine for it."

"Wonderful, I would love to see that."

Anne pointed toward a cabinet decorated with award ribbons. "Those are only some of the ribbons and medals the children from here have won."

"Now that truly is impressive!"

"We always get very excited when it's time for the Special Olympics. For the past two years people have approached me afterward about starting a school for special needs children."

"What an honor that must have been for you. What did you decide to do?"

"I agree with them that there is a need for such a school, but I don't have the time or resources to start one. If we have time later in our conversation, maybe I can tell you about my future dreams and plans for the children."

"I would enjoy hearing about that. Let's continue with your present needs and see if we have enough time for you to tell me about the future."

"Okay, well as you can see from this room, I use many different medical devices and medicines for the children. Those supplies often need to be replenished, along with toiletries and cleaning supplies. I also keep crayons, scissors, paper, and other craft supplies for the children in here. That's why this room is so full. Honestly, I usually don't invite people to my office because it's so cluttered."

"No problem, Anne. I can see how many people live here, so I know you have to have storage for everyone and everything. What is the highest number of children you have had living here, and how many do you have now?"

"The most I've ever had is thirty-three, and now we have twenty-seven."

"Oh my goodness! How did you move around with so many people living here? Where did everyone sleep?"

"Well, many of them were babies, so they didn't take up much room. Maybe you noticed that our cribs are large enough to easily contain two babies. We did have a few children sleeping on mats on the floor, but not many."

"So twenty-seven children live here now. How big is your home?"

"This is a three-bedroom apartment, but this room is used as an office and storage area, so we really only have two bedrooms. My bedroom is across the hall, and I share it with some of the children. Each night I will have at least three children in the bed with me. Having children in my bedroom gives everyone more space, and I try not to wake them up when I take care of the children in the other room throughout the night."

"Do you know what a saint is?"

"Yes, a good person."

"Well, I think you are a saint! For you to have left a very successful career and welcomed thirty-three children into your home and even to share your bed with them, I just can't imagine many other people in the world who would sacrifice themselves as you have done."

"Oh, I don't perceive this as a sacrifice, because I love the children. They need help and I can help them, so we are meant to be together. Many years ago when I first started volunteering with the city orphanage, I had a dream, and in my dream a baby with wings flew to me and asked me to take care of it, so I know I'm doing what I was meant to do."

"I know there are many people who are very thankful for your dream and your following through with it! Have you ever calculated how much you spend per month for each child on things like food, clothes, and toiletries?"

"Yes, I have. If you will give me a moment, I can tell you." Anne reached for a manila folder that was in a stack of folders about two feet high on her desk. To my surprise she was immediately able to find the information. "We spend a little over forty dollars a month on food for each child, a little over twenty dollars a month for clothes, and about fifteen dollars a month for toiletries and disinfectants. That's all in U.S. dollars."

"You seem very detail oriented. I guess that started with your career, and now it is especially a necessity for you." Anne laughed and nodded in agreement. I continued, "So tell me about your workers. How are they compensated?"

"I wish I could pay them more, but unfortunately all I can pay them is a little over three hundred dollars a month. I know that doesn't sound like much, but when you take into account the traditional annual bonus, it usually adds up to enough."

"Do you feel adequately staffed?"

"We get along sufficiently for what we can afford, but the workers have to perform many tasks. We ask them to wash clothes, feed babies, change diapers, keep watch, give medicine, dress the children, and keep them occupied."

"That is a full day. I'm sure they are very tired when they go home. How about your own bedroom and bathroom? Do you have any needs?"

"No, I'm just fine in that regard."

"What about the big room where the children play, do you have any needs there?"

"Our TV doesn't work well, and we need a better DVD player. Someone donated the wall cover that protects the bottom three feet of the wall, and the children like to look at the fish on it, so we don't need paint. The only computer we have is this desktop model, and I know it would help the children with their schoolwork if we had wi-fi and computers for them to use."

"Can you tell me if you have any dental care provided for the children?"

"There is a very nice dentist from the States named Philip. He comes here maybe two times a year and does free work for the children, and he's very playful with them."

"Tell me about the two storage areas near the entrance. Do you need anything for them?"

"The closet has built-in cabinets and I put some storage shelves in the open area, so all I need for it is to maybe sort, clean, and throw away some things. I like having the individually wrapped snacks for the children on the top storage shelf, because it's so easy to get to the snacks. The balcony desperately needs organizing. It was cluttered with a lot of different things. A couple of years ago, a man from the States who owns a construction company took almost everything out, bought some storage racks and assembled them, and then put the clutter back. But he (and others) have told me that I need to go through all of the things I have stored throughout the apartment and discard what I don't use. But I would hate the idea of throwing out anything that I spent money to purchase, so I keep everything."

"I mean no disrespect, but I agree that you should throw some things away. I don't know how you find everything you need, and I would be afraid to go out on the storage balcony. I don't know what's in the boxes, but a bike, stroller, or sporting equipment could fall on you. Do you need anything in the kitchen?"

"Yes. A few months ago our refrigerator stopped working and we lost all our food, because it was a holiday weekend and nobody was available to service the refrigerator. It took two weeks for someone to finally find some parts for it. They told me that the refrigerator is so old that it's too challenging and expensive to repair it further, so I guess we will need a new refrigerator soon. The man who assembled the storage shelves on the balcony gave me some suggestions about remodeling the kitchen. He thinks if we move the door, we can free up some counter space, and we could also move the refrigerator to the same side as the sink and stove."

Anne continued, "The other thing I would like most for the kitchen is a dishwasher, because right now I don't have any way to sterilize our dishes; and when one child gets sick, they all get sick. Also, right now we have a two-burner propane stovetop and we cook in a wok, but I have seen some great ovens. I think they would give us many more options how to cook for the children, and maybe we could provide them with healthier food. And the man with the construction company said if we raised the suspended ceiling, we could add taller cabinets, which would give me more storage. Additionally, he suggested replacing the tile walls and broken countertop."

I paused from writing down the many requests for the kitchen while Anne and I talked about some of the children's physical challenges. Of course, I knew that some of them needed to use strollers or crutches to get around, and I'd noticed that they had trouble with other tasks as well. I wondered how Anne got them to school and their various appointments.

I took up my notebook again as Anne continued her brainstorm: "I've seen something called a stander in a magazine, and it looks like it would help the children with tethered spine syndrome and cerebral palsy. The stander would help a disabled child to stand and be supported. You can even get them with trays for working or eating."

"That sounds like something that would be very beneficial for Qing Qing and Ming Ming! Is there anything else that comes to mind?"

"Well, on days when it rains or snows, we have more trouble getting the children to school because we have to wait outside in the weather for a taxi. It truly would be nice to have a van. Also, when we have a medical emergency or when we take several children in for their shots, it would serve us well and would save the money that we would otherwise spend on taxis."

"I agree. That makes perfect sense. Do you have a driver's license?"

"Yes, I have a driver's license. Did you know that it costs much more to get a driver's license in China than it does in the States?"

"Yes, some of my students told me that. Do you have time to tell me about other needs that may not be material or are only 'big dreams' for now?"

"Sure. I have some extra help today. It would be wonderful to have more workers here on a regular basis so we could provide even better care for the children and keep the apartment cleaner. You know, the floor is always sticky where the children play because they spill things, pee on the floor, and walk on it constantly. I know when people visit for the first time they don't understand all of the activity on that floor, so I would like to have it mopped a couple of times each day, but we don't seem to be able to accomplish that. In my dreams I would like to provide a physical therapist for some of the children. We have three children with cerebral palsy, and two of them would be great candidates for the standers we talked about earlier. The other child with cerebral palsy, John, can only lie on his bed and doesn't move much at all, but he responds well to being moved or touched."

I remembered John and how he smiled when his wheelchair was turned toward the sun during the trip to the park. That was the first time I had seen him smile, and it made me wonder whether he had a lot more awareness than he could easily express.

Anne continued, "We have had a couple of volunteers who were physical therapists or nurses, and when they would move John around, he would smile. He also likes it when we cut his fingernails, so he's like the other children in that he likes attention."

"That makes sense. Do the other children pay him any attention?"

"No, they don't really know what to do with him and they get too busy playing, so John doesn't get much activity during the day."

"Ah, that's sad. Hopefully he enjoys the commotion going on around him all the time. What other dreams do you have for the children?"

"Well, in addition to a physical therapist, I would like to have a speech therapist. You know, many of the children who come to me with a cleft palate have the surgeries they need, but they could still use some help afterwards. Even though Paul is the oldest boy here, sometimes the children and teachers have to ask him to repeat himself because he has a bit of a speech impediment since his cleft palate was so severe."

"I am thankful you mentioned Paul because I've been thinking about his inability to get his registration. Oh, what is the word I was taught for that card everyone needs? Is it a Hukou?"

"Ah, very good job with remembering the Chinese word!"

"Thanks. Believe me, I'm surprised I remembered it and that you could understand me when I said it. From what Holly and Lizzy told me about Paul's situation, it sounds like his inability to get his Hukou could haunt him the rest of his life. It's tragic that he was never registered in his home province before you received him."

"Yes, his situation is troublesome for me. There was a really nice American woman who had come to China a couple of times, and she would volunteer here. She even brought her sister and some of their friends. They did many activities with the children, and the children loved spending time with them. The woman wanted to adopt Paul, so she brought her husband here to meet him. We had a good visit and talked about how they could adopt him. When they went home, they started working with an adoption agency, which I'm told requires quite a lot of time and money on the adopting family's part. Well, they completed all of their paper-work, had their home inspected, had background checks done on themselves, and then were only waiting on me. I had completed all of the paperwork that I could do for Paul, but he wasn't registered. In China, a child who isn't registered can't be processed for adoption.

"Since I wasn't making any real progress, I tried to get my friends at the city orphanage to help, and they told me what I already knew: that his registration would probably have to be done in Paul's home province. I have a friend who works with the government there so I went to see him, explained Paul's situation, and gave him all of the paperwork. He was at the director's level, so I knew that if I had any chance at all of getting Paul a Hukou, it would be through this man. He assured me that he would try to help, and he knew there was a loving family waiting for Paul with open arms. It truly would have been a great situation because the family had already raised three boys, and two of them were twins, which the Chinese consider lucky. Also, the lady's brother had adopted multiple children from China, so Paul would have Chinese cousins.

"Time was dragging on, and I'm sure the family wanting to adopt Paul was growing tired of the situation. I kept contacting the man in Paul's home province to get updates on his progress, but there was none. After a very long wait, the man finally told me that although there were times when it was easier to get something like this registration accomplished, unfortunately, this wasn't one of them. I felt so sorry for the Americans who wanted to adopt Paul, because they had done everything they could. Their adoption agency was waiting for his name to appear on the list of children to be matched, but it never happened. They had done so much paperwork and spent so much money, not to mention the emotional rollercoaster they had endured. I also felt sorry because Paul's fate had been sealed. After my friend from Paul's home province said he couldn't help, I didn't think Paul would ever be able to receive his Hukou."

"Did you tell Paul that the family wanted to adopt him, so he would at least have the satisfaction of knowing there were people who wanted to welcome him into their family and share their home and lives with him?"

"No. When the husband and wife came together so the husband could meet Paul, we didn't tell Paul why there were here. We didn't make a huge deal out of it, and Paul had seen the lady here before, so I don't think he made any assumptions. We knew it was going to be hard to get Paul's papers in order, and I didn't want him to be disappointed."

"I can certainly understand how you would want to protect Paul from disappointment, and I know you weighed that against the joy he could have knowing someone wanted to adopt him. Wow, I wouldn't want to be you for a day!"

"This system we use in China must be a little hard for you to understand, and I can see why. Some people who knew how we were struggling to get Paul's registration suggested I go to the province and find an official who would be willing to help get the documentation for Paul if I offered a nice tip. I don't like that system of getting things done, and I knew the people who wanted to adopt Paul had integrity, so I refused that option."

"Anne, the more I get to know you, the more I appreciate the struggles you face. You are loving toward the children and sometimes you have to make difficult decisions. I admire and respect you, and though I don't understand all of your challenges, I know that you walked away from your successful career to provide a home for these unwanted children. They are loved and fed under your care, and they call you Mama, so that is the bottom line for me."

"Thank you! You know, just hearing that periodically keeps me motivated, because I do feel like I'm on an island. Foreigners don't understand the problems we have in certain areas, and many

Chinese people don't want to see orphans, especially orphans with special needs, so my job can be lonely."

I could see that it was painful for Anne to talk about these challenges, so I changed the subject and asked about her hopes for the future.

Anne leaned back in her chair and gazed at the ceiling, deep in thought for a few moments. Then she looked back at me and smiled wistfully. "I would like to have a nursery school for children with special needs. Then once I get a good process in place and some proven policies, I would like to expand into other provinces, and the schools could generate money to help the children with their other needs."

"That certainly is an ambitious goal, and it sounds like you have put some thought into it. Do you remember how you initially came up with this idea?"

"Sure, I remember. There were many foreigners working in our city a few years ago, and they volunteered here. They were a diverse group from Canada, England, the Philippines, Germany, Australia, and the States. To my surprise, they raised the money to have a home built for us that would have been perfect for the school. I have the deed and all of the documents showing that I own the house free and clear. I keep them in the largest notebook in the bookshelf to the right of the window. The documents have the chop, or official stamp, so it's all authenticated."

"Why didn't you move forward with starting your school when you received the funding?"

"The home had to be built, so that took time, and while the home was being built, one by one the foreigners went back to their homelands before anything was done to the interior."

I couldn't believe donors would begin a project like this and then abandon it midstream. "Is there any way you can complete the house?"

"There are a few reasons for my lack of progress. The first one is money. I can't afford to finish it."

"How much it would it cost?"

"About \$120,000 in US dollars. Two architects from the States have looked at it, and they agree about what needs to be done and how much it would cost."

"I can see how the need for money would slow your progress. What else has been an impediment?"

"The house was built outside the city in a very nice new neighborhood with free-standing homes, not apartment buildings like we have in the cities, so we would have our own yard with apple trees. But because it's a gated up-and-coming neighborhood, my application to open a nursery school for children with special needs was rejected by the Civil Administration Bureau. I understand why my school wouldn't be wanted there now, but I think in a few years as the city continues to expand, maybe it will be approved."

"Please don't think I am being disrespectful, but have you thought about selling the house and using the cash for the things you mentioned earlier?"

"Yes, I have thought about that, but I'm holding on to the dream of being able to help many families with special needs children by providing an excellent nursery school for them. If I ever do sell the house, I think I would try to get a first-floor apartment in the city. A first-floor apartment would make things easier for the children with mobility challenges."

"You must have a wonderful board of directors that helps you plan the future for the children and yourself."

"I like to think I do, and it's multi-national. We also have a medical advisor, an American medical professional who was adopted herself. She gives us good advice about the children's health care."

"All of these medical procedures, tests, and operations cost so much money. How do you pay for all of it and keep the orphanage going?"

"It was easier in the past when the international church in Hong Kong gave us more money, but we do the best we can. A successful businessman from Australia was volunteering here and he now generously supports us, and so does his church in Australia. He adopted a boy from our orphanage, and the boy is now in college."

"Wow, that is a success story! So the boy went from being abandoned because of a medical issue, to living in your orphanage, to being adopted by what I can only imagine is a good family in Australia, and now he's in college! That is great. Stories like that must make you feel wonderful."

"Yes, I'm very thankful for how well the boy's life has turned out."

"So from where else do you receive money for taking care of the children?"

"There are some foreigners in town who give some, but that isn't very consistent, and there is a nonprofit organization in the States that also helps."

"Do local people and local churches contribute?"

"A couple of small local churches contribute, but not much and not often. Occasionally local individuals donate to us, but you need to understand that until fairly recently, few people in China had discretionary money to give. Two things have recently begun to change the way Chinese people view giving to help others: one is our growing economy, and the other is the enormous earthquake that hit the Wenchuan area of Sichuan Province in 2008. That horrible event gave people in China something to donate to, and since then people have slowly become more favorable to the idea of donating money. I imagine that previously, most Chinese would have told you that the only charitable organization they had ever heard of was the Red Cross."

"I'm surprised to hear you say that as a rule Chinese people haven't been generous in giving in the past, because my experience has been just the opposite. So many students have given me gifts, and some have given me gifts from their parents."

"You're different, because you're a foreigner and their teacher. Also, students are young, and the younger generation is more open to contributing to needs than the older generations. The older generations have had so many financial struggles, it's understandable that they don't give as freely. The college students today have seen our economy explode, so they have more resources from which to give."

"I can't imagine how you manage to budget with all of the unexpected medical expenses."

"Yes, that remains consistently problematic. I can't imagine a month without at least one child having a surprise medical expense. It does make it hard to adhere to a budget, but one thing that helps is that this is my home—and it's completely paid for—so there's no rent. The board of directors is advising me that the orphanage should pay me some amount of rent, but I wouldn't feel comfortable taking rent from them. I know the board members are wise and good people, so we'll see how that plays out."

"You are so generous to the children. The more I learn, the more I understand that about you. I also notice that on your list of needs, there is nothing for yourself. Do you have a plan with your board of directors about retiring someday?"

"Yes, I have a succession plan. I have legally adopted one of the girls here, and the plan is that she will assume my role when I retire. Currently she is in the States going to school. A friend of a friend knew about an organization that gives children scholarships to study abroad, so they are paying for her tuition at a private school, and she is living with a nice family who agreed to assist. Once she finishes college, we plan on her coming back and leading the orphanage."

"Amazing. I didn't know about your adopted daughter. I hope she could speak English before she went to school in the States.

You've obviously done a wonderful job of instilling great values in her if she's willing to return to the orphanage to lead it after she receives her education."

"That's our current plan, and so far we are on schedule. Yes, she could speak English before she went to school there. I can't imagine how hard her transition would have been if she couldn't speak the language. She does miss the children and the food here, but she also enjoys her new friends and pizza."

"Good for her, and I think pizza is universally enjoyed as an awesome food." This seemed like a good stopping point for our conversation, so I closed my notepad and put my pen in my purse.

"Well," I said, "I feel like I've taken up so much of your time today. I appreciate how busy you are and how generous you have been with your time, so I think I will leave you for now. I do want to assure you that even though I'm returning to the States, I want to help you. I don't know to what extent that will be, but you and the children will forever be on my mind and heart. Thanks so much for the way you have loved, provided for, and cared for the children. I can't imagine where they would be without you!"

12

THE ASK

After meeting with Anne, I was determined to do what I could for her and the children before returning to the States. Because I had spent so much time at the orphanage rather than sightseeing and shopping as I had originally planned, I had enough funds to make a substantial gift, and I wanted to pick something to buy from Anne's list. But I was going to need some help, so I called Holly. "Holly, this is Jan. How are you today?"

"I'm doing well. Hopefully you can say the same for yourself."

"Yes, I'm doing great! I have lots on my plate as I'm getting ready to go back home, but I have a crazy question for you. Would you be able to take me someplace where I can buy a refrigerator?"

Holly laughed so hard, she said tears were streaming down her face. "Jan, you have always had an ability to make me laugh, but this question completely caught me off guard. What in heaven's name will you do with a refrigerator? If the one in your room broke, you're not responsible for it and don't need to replace it. Oh, what a hoot your call is for me."

"The refrigerator isn't for my room, it's for Anne and the children. Anne told me that hers broke not too long ago, and that they lost everything they had stored in it. There was a delay in getting it repaired because it was so old and parts couldn't easily be found, so I want to buy one for them before I leave. I have enough cash to do that and still get home, but I need someone to go with me to help me make a good selection, and arrange for it to be delivered and for the old one to be removed. I would never be able to negotiate all of that in Chinese."

"What a nice gesture!" Holly said. "I do remember when their refrigerator stopped working. They had an awful, smelly mess on their hands. You and I have done an enormous amount of shopping together, but never in my wildest imagination did I ever think I would go to the refrigerator department with you! When would you like to go?"

"Since I don't have much time left here, the sooner the better, but I don't want you to rearrange your schedule for me."

"Nonsense, you are doing something very kind for my friends, so I will do all I can to assist all of you. Besides, I may want to do a little more shopping than just for refrigerators."

"Oh, I see. This will be one of those retail therapy trips for us! I love shopping with you; I always see so many extra things I wouldn't have noticed alone, and you teach me some history too."

"And I enjoy getting out of the house most days, so this is a wonderful reason to go somewhere. Would tomorrow morning at nine o'clock work for you?"

"Sure, but only if you didn't have anything planned."

"No, it's fine. Nine o'clock it is, and I will have a driver meet us at the south gate of the campus."

"Sounds great. Thanks."

My day passed quickly as I worked through my to-do list in preparation for my departure. Thankfully I didn't have as much to pack as I did on my previous trip. I was preoccupied with my work, so lunchtime passed before I realized what time it was. Finally I went to the street to get something to eat, and sure enough, my favorite street vendor was there at her cart, making her delicious wraps. I had bought food from her so often she knew how I wanted mine cooked, with an egg and with no oil added to the pan when she browned the outside. I couldn't believe I could still get a wrap for less than a dollar.

I had arranged to Skype with my team at work after dinner. During my stay in China, I had been sharing with everyone on the team about the orphans, and I had told my assistant, Mark, about my plan to ask them to help me raise money for Xiao Ting's operation. We decided that I would ask everyone at the same time via Skype on the big-screen TV in the conference room.

After the team and I talked through some business, I asked Mark if he had received the video I sent him from the orphanage along with some photos. He said that he had, and that he had shown them to everyone. The video was of three-year-old Xiao Ting feeding a baby and doing it well. Xiao Ting held a stainless steel bowl and was scooping food into the baby's mouth with a small spoon. When the baby turned his head and some of the food got on his face, Xiao Ting carefully spooned it up and tried again to scoop it into his mouth. It was an amazing and precious thing to watch.

I addressed the group in the conference room: "I appreciate all of you taking time to watch the video and look at the pictures I've sent. The little girl in the video feeding the baby is my little buddy Xiao Ting. When I go to the orphanage she meets me at the door along with the other children, and she gives me a huge smile and raises her arms so I will pick her up. If I sit down, she crawls in my lap and we look at a book, and then she points out things in the pictures and tells me all about them.

"Well, this darling little girl has a hole in her heart, which causes her lips and fingertips to turn blue. She needs an operation to repair her heart, but the doctors have been waiting for her to grow and become stronger. Recently, however, she fainted at the orphanage, and now the doctors say they can't wait any longer. This operation will cost over $8,000, and in China such procedures must be paid for in advance. The leader of the orphanage hasn't received her normal contributions, so she doesn't have the cash on hand to pay for the procedure."

My heart was pounding as I prepared to request the team's help. I was worried about how they would receive my request and whether it would have any impact on our relationship. But I had to set my personal feelings aside because my little buddy needed the operation. So I dived right in: "I have decided to try to raise enough money for Xiao Ting's surgery, and I'm asking all of you to consider helping." I waited for a few awkward moments while nobody said a word, then continued. "I'll be in the office before the end of next week. I'm looking forward to seeing all of you again, and we can talk more about Xiao Ting and her operation then. Now I'm sure Mark wants you to direct your attention to work, so thanks again for listening and for considering helping."

I can't describe how strongly I wanted to find a hole and hide in it after making my request. I am not at all the type to ask my friends for money, even for a great cause. I began wondering whether they would avoid me at work now, especially given that haunting silence after I asked! For the time being, though, I needed to concentrate on buying the new refrigerator and preparing for my return to the States.

13

MODERN CONVENIENCES

Holly met me at the south gate the next morning and immediately spotted our driver, who was waving at us. Her ease in finding drivers never ceased to amaze me. "How many people do you know who drive?" I asked her. "It seems like some of the drivers we've used are friends of yours."

"Several are, but I haven't counted how many. I try to use a couple of drivers most often, and then distribute my remaining business among the remaining drivers I know. Our driver today is very proud of his new VW. He believes that because it was manufactured by a German company it's made well and will last him many miles."

"It certainly does look like a new car, and what a shine on it! I wonder how long he can keep it looking so nice."

"Knowing him as I do, I think he will do an excellent job of maintaining the new shine as long as he can. He was an accountant for the university before he retired and started his driving business to supplement his retirement income. I'll go ahead and warn you that he and I will be speaking in Chinese about our old comrades, so you may feel excluded from our conversation. I wanted to apologize in advance."

"No problem. Enjoy your visit while I take in the scenery."

"Funny you should mention that. We're actually going to an area of town you've probably never seen. We'll go where builders and remodelers buy their supplies. I think you'll receive a significantly better price there than at one of the large department stores. My husband knows a man working there, so he called him for you last night. He verified that he would be there today, and he knows you're doing this for the orphans, so he's agreed to give you a large discount."

"Wonderful! That's so nice of him to provide a discount. I like him already."

Holly was correct: I had never seen this section of the city. Many large trucks were on the streets, and the businesses didn't have colorful storefronts; they looked more industrial. Holly seemed to enjoy her chat with the driver, who was a very interesting-looking man with thick, bushy eyebrows. He smiled often while they spoke, and nodded frequently. For some reason, I felt sure he would be a fantastic grandfather. Maybe I just liked his smile and the way he was engaging Holly in conversation, but I was thinking about how great he would be with the children who lived with Anne.

As usual, when we reached our destination, Holly and I debated about whose turn it was to pay the taxi (which was an argument she almost always won). Either she would say that she had the driver for the day because she would be running errands afterward; or she would be sitting up front because she knew the driver, and would already have her money out and hand it to the driver before I could lean forward and see the meter. This time was like almost every other, so I resigned myself to letting Holly pay and we climbed out of the taxi.

"This is the best store in our little city for purchasing refrigerators," she explained. "If we walk to the back of the store, on the right side, we'll find them."

"Do you come here often enough to know where all of the merchandise is?"

"No, my husband asked his friend when he spoke to him."

"You're so logical. I should have known you had some good way of knowing, and I'm thankful you do because this store is huge!"

"Yes, it is very large. With our economy growing, people have money for nice new things like refrigerators."

As we approached the refrigerator department, a very professional looking man wearing shiny leather shoes, dark colored slacks, and a plaid shirt greeted us with a friendly "Ni hao." Holly answered his greeting, and we shook hands with him. The two of them talked briefly and then, to my surprise, he turned around and walked off.

Holly explained, "He suggested we look around first and find a few refrigerators that we think have potential for meeting Anne's needs. Once we have a short list, we can find him and ask him any questions we have about each one."

"That sounds like a good plan to me. Did he tell you where we should start?"

"Well, what type of refrigerator do you want?"

"I think stainless steel would be appropriate for them because it would be durable, stylish, and easy to clean. What do you think?"

"Yes, I agree." Holly said. "I can see some shiny refrigerators beyond that atrocious blue one to our right."

"I see them too, so let's have a look!" I was surprised by how excited I was to be finding the perfect refrigerator for Anne and the children, and my pace quickened. As I scanned the selection, my eyes were drawn to one particular model. I called Holly over to see it. "Look, this even has an in-door ice and water dispenser. The refrigerator section is on top, and the freezer is below with a pullout drawer. The shelf configuration is adjustable and so are the pockets in the doors."

"I don't know," Holly said, frowning. "It may be too wide for the space available in the kitchen."

"Well, I secretly paced off the old one so we could make sure to buy one that would fit, because I want this to be a surprise for Anne. When you speak to your friend about the price, please remember to have him add in the delivery and removal charges. I don't want Anne to have to worry with anything or any expenses. I don't know yet if this one will work. I searched for refrigerators online, and it looks like this type of model would cost about $3,000 in the States. If it's that high here, I can't afford it."

Holly waved to the salesman and got his attention. He quickly approached us and spoke with Holly, then went to his desk and returned with a clipboard. After looking at a chart on the clipboard, he quoted a price to Holly.

Holly turned to me, smiling broadly, "I don't know if this refrigerator is just less expensive in China or if he's giving you a huge discount, but the total price including delivery of the new unit and removal of Anne's old refrigerator is only $857 US dollars."

"That's amazing! Oh, he's a wonderful man. Now I can afford to completely stock the new refrigerator. This is awesome. I am very excited about this purchase!"

"I am too. He says this model is very popular, and the shipment wouldn't be here for a week. If you want a model like this right away, they have one he can sell you for a little less, but it has a few scratches on it."

"I don't mind waiting for an unscratched one. I wanted it delivered after I leave town so it can be a little farewell surprise for Anne and the children. Do you think you would be able to let Anne know it's coming? And if I give you the money, would you stock it for them?"

"Sure, that won't be a problem. You know, each morning there's a market on the street beside the park, so the morning of the delivery I can purchase a lot of meat for them, then put it in the new freezer."

"Great idea! This whole deal is working out much better than I imagined, but I couldn't have done it without you!"

"Nonsense, you could have done this without me. You're a big international businesswoman now, so this would have been easy for you to navigate." We both laughed, because we knew I would have never been able to speak enough Chinese to accomplish this, nor would I have known about this area of town or had a connection for a discount.

Holly's friend returned with the paperwork. I counted out the money and gave it to him. I then asked Holly to tell him to keep the change and use it to buy his lunch, since he was so kind to us and gave me such a wonderful discount.

Holly relayed the message, and the salesman answered and pointed to another area of the store. Holly burst into laughter, and he did as well. He walked off with the cash and quickly returned with my change.

"I thought I was buying him lunch, so why did he bring me change? And what were you laughing about?"

"He said he would return your change because there's a new vendor in the microwave department who has food out as samples, so he had already planned to eat for free."

"He is truly thrifty, so I like how he thinks." I gave Holly some more of the cash I had brought. "Here is money for stocking the refrigerator. Thanks so much for all your help."

"No need to thank me," Holly said graciously. "I enjoy helping my friends."

"Please don't tell Anne until after I've left for home! You said you wanted to run errands today, but I think I will go by the orphanage for a little while before I do some work in my room. Would you help me hail a taxi and tell the driver where to take me?"

"Sure. No problem. On your way there you need to call Lizzy. She has something interesting to tell you, and if you call her on your way to the orphanage, she should have time in her schedule to speak with you."

We hailed a taxi and once I was settled in, I called Lizzy. She asked how the refrigerator shopping had gone.

"It went great! Holly's husband knows a guy who works there, and he gave us an amazing deal since we're helping the orphans."

"Yeah, Holly told me what you were doing, so I wanted to thank you for helping our little friends."

"I'm thankful to be able to do a little something to help, Lizzy. I'm calling because Holly said you have something interesting to tell me."

"Yes, I certainly do. Do you remember the students we were friends with at the English Corner?"

"Sure. In fact, I'm still in touch with some of them."

"Well, I started getting some of them to communicate with the orphans from the fire at the fireworks factory. We even took a bus out to the rural village to meet them, and now they are acting as mentors for the orphans and helping them learn English. I meant to tell you about this after we had our visit with the three children soon after you arrived, but we got so busy visiting Anne's orphanage that I forgot to fill you in. I thought telling you about it now as you're about to head home would be a nice good-bye gift."

"It certainly is! What are some of the things the college students have done with the children?"

"Many interesting things. During Christmas, they told the children to whom they'd been assigned about how English-speaking cultures celebrate that holiday. Also they asked the younger students what they would like for a gift, since that is part of the Christmas celebration. You would be floored by the responses we received. I cried when I read them because they were so humbling, touching, and sweet. One child said she wanted a blouse for her eighty-two-year-old grandmother whom she lives with. Another child said he would like a pair of glasses so he could see the board at school. Other answers included a ball, some fruit, and school supplies."

There was an unusual moment of silence between Lizzy and me. I was stunned. The children asked for so little, and some of them even requested gifts for others and not for themselves—such a contrast with many children in the States, whose wish lists would be vastly different.

"Lizzy, thanks so much for sharing that with me. It gives me a new perspective on how fortunate I am. Wow, it will take me quite some time to get my mind around that list you received, and I'm so thankful to know that because of the college students we are helping the children in yet another way. What a wonderful idea you had about getting people from the English Corner to help."

"I can't take all of the credit for that. Holly helped, and then she got the ladies auxiliary to provide the bus that took us to meet them. We all pitch in and do what we can, and we appreciate how you have continued to send support even though you no longer reside here."

"Well, after hearing that list, I feel like I should contribute more!"

"You're doing plenty, and we appreciate it. So, how are you doing with your departure plans? Are your flights arranged?"

"Yes, all of my travel plans are complete, and I have accomplished everything I was supposed to for work, so I only have a few loose ends to tie up, and then I will be ready to go."

"One of Holly's driver friends has a nice van, so maybe Holly and I could take you to the bus station, and we would have room in the van for your luggage."

"Now that sounds lovely, and I will be sure to mention it to Holly."

14

HELP

I had let Anne know that I would be stopping by one last time before returning to the States. I hoped that she would be able to answer a few more questions to help round out my picture of the orphanage, so I could answer my co-workers' queries when I talked with them about contributing for Xiao Ting's surgery. Fortunately, because many of the children were at school, Anne was able to take a few more minutes with me this time.

My first question was about something that had been bothering me ever since Lizzy and Holly told me about Paul and his need for a Hukou: "I have heard that once orphans turn fourteen, they are supposed to leave the orphanage. Who takes care of them at that young age, and what do they do?"

"Well, technically that is correct," Anne answered, "but it doesn't happen often. The officials are much too busy to try to keep up with every orphan's age and date of birth, and the orphanages don't want to remove anyone that young out of their care. But for the children who are approaching adulthood, I've found a program in our city that will accept young people and let them live there while they learn a skill. This gives the children time to become more mature, and once they complete the program they have a marketable skill. I also know of a school that teaches special needs orphans a skill, and they also let the children live at the school. It's a kind of medical school where they teach physical therapy, massage, and related subjects."

"That's good to know. I can't imagine a fourteen-year-old being on the streets alone."

"I understand your thoughts, but unfortunately it does happen sometimes."

"Where do children in such a situation go, and what do they do?"

"They might get a low-level job and share an apartment with several people. You know, in China we aren't as strict as it is in America, when it comes to the age of someone working."

"I'm sorry to tell you this, but I keep thinking of questions for you. So would you mind if I asked more?"

"That will be fine. What are you interested in knowing about today?"

"Well, I was wondering about the little boy who looks like he's about seven or eight years old. There is another boy about the same age, and they are inseparable. They are a little rougher than the other children, and when the boy I am talking about falls down, he doesn't get up. I've seen the other children get behind him, wrap their arms around his chest, and help him up, and then he runs and plays like nothing happened until he falls again. He runs and plays so hard, so why can't he get up by himself?"

"Yes, he does play hard and that causes him to fall often. He has a disease called Duchenne muscular dystrophy; maybe you have heard it called Duchenne syndrome. The doctors tell me he has textbook symptoms of the disease, because his legs are weak and his calves are very large. Unfortunately, the doctors say he probably won't live past twenty-five, because he will lose control of his arm and neck muscles, and then paralysis will follow."

"That is a horrible-sounding disease. I'm so sorry to hear about his prognosis. Please don't think less of me for asking this, but have you ever had a child die while in your care?"

"Not here, but once I was given an abandoned child in another province who was in terrible condition due to a heart problem. I took the child to a local hospital, and they did all they could for him, but they said that his best chance for survival would be at a larger hospital because they didn't have a surgeon who could do the operation he needed. They made arrangements for us to fly to Beijing, where he could receive care at a better hospital. As we were landing, the child passed out, so I obviously got him to the hospital as quickly as I could. Within two hours of arriving at the hospital, he died. Whenever I receive a call telling me to come and get an abandoned child, that tragedy is what motivates me, because that child might have lived if we could have gotten him better medical attention more quickly."

"I'm so sorry you experienced that."

"Well, his death was peaceful because he had fainted. Maybe it was best that I hadn't known him for more than a couple of days, but I was still numb after he died."

"I'm sure you were, and I'm so sorry. I also want you to ask about a couple of the girls. When they were wrestling around on the floor, they pulled up each other's shirts in the back, and I noticed that each girl has a scar along their spine. What caused that? The two girls seem perfectly healthy."

"Oh, they have spina bifida, but they don't have tethered spine syndrome, so they can walk. The scar is where a sack of fluid was on their spine before being removed surgically. They don't have any limitations, but we do have to monitor where the incision was. If it ever looks like one of the girls is retaining fluid again, we will have to get medical attention quickly."

"I'm glad to know that they seem to have no lingering effects from the spina bifida. Good for them!"

"The taller of the two girls does well in school, too. She has done a wonderful job of picking up English words, so maybe in a few years she will be able to communicate with you in English. Oh, and she loves to talk on the phone. Sometimes I go into the office and she's holding the phone to her head and carrying on a conversation with an imaginary person."

"You will have your hands full with her if she's already acting like a teenager!"

"Please, don't remind me!"

Anne changed three diapers while we sat there talking about the children, orphanages in China, raising support, and her own challenges, all while playing with the children as well. I knew I would be leaving this loving environment soon, so I wanted to absorb all I could. The playful, smiling faces; the smells of the orphanage; and yes, even the sticky floor. I could hear Anne's brother-in-law in the kitchen cooking, and I watched a worker hanging the laundry to dry on a rack indoors. I watched Anne lovingly attend to the children, and I wondered about the source of her compassion. Perhaps over time I would learn more of her story, but for now it was time for me to go.

"Anne, I don't think I'll see you and the children again before I go back to the States, so I want to sincerely thank you for the way you have given so much of yourself for them. I admire you and your willingness to sacrifice for them. We need more people like you in the world. Thank you for opening your home to me and letting me enjoy your huge family!"

"Thank you for being interested in the children," Anne responded graciously. "I'm always willing to welcome good people who want to spend time with them, and thanks for your pledge to raise the support for Xiao Ting's operation. Some of the children here have seizures, so I'm accustomed to seeing that, but it definitely scared me when she fainted."

"Well, we don't want that to happen again, so I've already told some friends back home about her condition and needs. Hopefully I'll have some good news for you shortly after I get home. I'll wire you the funds when I have them. Thanks for your time today, and I'll definitely be in touch."

15

UNEXPECTED GREAT NEWS

As I arrived at my workplace for my first day back after my trip to China, it dawned on me that I didn't know where to sit. My assistant Mark, who was also replacing me in my former role, had moved into my old office. I stopped by and saw that he had done a great job of decorating the space—the walls were covered with his photography and posters about leadership. I left him a note saying that the office looked amazing and that I wanted to chat with him when he had time, then I made my way to David's office to discuss my new position.

"Good morning, David."

"Ni hao!"

"Oh my gosh, you've started speaking Chinese since I left! That is awesome!"

"Ha! I think you know I haven't picked up a new language, but I did find out how to say hello in Chinese. Do you have a few minutes to talk?"

"Sure. You have my undivided attention."

"First of all, let me compliment you on the work you did in China. I know my directions for you were somewhat vague, but you had the vision to fine-tune your approach and provided us with some amazing articles."

"Thank you."

"Between your experience in China and your work ethic, we think you're the right person for a new role in the company. What we envision for you is a hybrid position that would enable you to continue the work you were doing before your assignment there, and you would be responsible for managing our international work as well. Mark and his team would report directly to you, as would six other teams."

"Can you tell me more about the international side of these new responsibilities?"

"Well, while you were away, we not only printed your articles in our periodical, but we also published them on a new blog the IT department created for you. This was an experiment to gauge interest in the type of information you were reporting and the use of technology to communicate it. We used a small amount of resources to promote the blog on social media, and IT helped with search engine optimization, so your articles received traction immediately. We were so impressed with the growth of people visiting the blog and subscribing that we knew there was a future in this. Jan, you obviously have an uncanny ability to find stories that are fascinating to the public, and you present them in a manner that draws people in, and we want to capitalize on that. So not only do we want you to continue traveling in China, we want you to train a team to do the same things you are doing. Once you have prepared a team of journalists, we can send them around the world; and if they are as successful as you have been, it will strengthen our core business. You did a masterful job of hand-selecting your old team, which Mark now leads, so we want you to do the same with your international team."

"I'm very flattered by your words, David. I assure you that I will do everything I can to affirm the decision you and senior management made to honor me with this incredible opportunity!"

"There's more. We noticed the enhancements you provided to the university's website in China when you were working on that special project for your former dean, so we also want you to be on the team that creates our new online presence. You won't be the leader of this team, but we certainly want you to play a significant role in developing our new way of presenting ourselves digitally. The people on this team will be our best and brightest because we see so much potential for our company to go global."

"Thank you for considering me worthy to serve with that team. I'm sure everyone is eager to begin."

"So you are up for this new role?"

"Absolutely!"

"Terrific. Then we need to take care of some housekeeping details. You will use Mary's old office. Hopefully that will be suitable for you. Jodi will talk with you about the spending allowance for sprucing up your new office. I've also scheduled a meeting for you with Lance from HR to review your job description, and he will present your compensation package. I think you will be pleased with the arrangements we have made for you. If you have any questions for me, please let me know. Finally, I want to make sure you are aware that we see your position as fluid, so if we need to make adjustments, we will. Now if you'll excuse me, I have a conference call in about one minute."

I thanked David, checked in with Jodi about the decorating budget, then walked down the hall to my new office. I was looking out the window when Lance walked in. "Nice view, huh?"

It startled me, but then I turned and greeted my colleague. "Oh, good morning Lance. Yes, it's a wonderful view of the lake and trees!"

"Are you ready to go over some documents with me, or should I come back later?"

"No, this is a good time for me."

We sat on opposite sides of my new desk, and Lance pulled out a large folder and pushed it across the desk toward me.

"Unfortunately, one thing I'm lacking for you is a title," he said. "Your position is new and intersects with several departments within the company, so the title is yet to be decided."

"No problem. That's completely understandable."

"Thanks for understanding. I think you'll be pleased with the rest of what I have to tell you. As you learned from your meeting with David, you will have many responsibilities within our company, so finding an exact match to get the industry range for your new salary was impossible." He opened the folder and tapped a sheet of paper with his index finger. "As you can see on this compensation form, your new salary will be more than twice your old one. Also, David was able to get you options on a quarterly basis, plus a one-time deal of two thousand options in recognition of your promotion. You can either cash out these options or save them for as long as you desire."

I was stunned by the generosity of the offer. "Thank you so much, Lance. I'm honored by the trust you've placed in me. I'm fortunate to be a small part of the company and the new direction it's taking."

"Our pleasure. You've done good work for us," he said. "Please take some time to look over the job description and let me know right away if you have any questions." As he stood to leave, he asked, "Has anyone told you about lunch today?"

"No, what's going on?"

"David wanted to have an informal lunch with your old team, those who are interested in China, and those who have played a role in creating your new position. Many people are interested in the opportunities abroad, and we all feel that China is a fantastic location to focus on initially."

"That sounds great. Will you be at the lunch?"

"Yes, I was invited. Oh, and David is insisting that everyone try to use chop sticks with the Chinese food he's ordered."

"That should be entertaining! I'll see you there."

The morning flew by as I set up my office and met with several of the team leaders who would be reporting to me. Then I headed to lunch in the conference room.

When I arrived, the others were already there, including David. A caterer had set up some very large stainless steel serving bowls full of Chinese food along the tables, just like they do in China. We filled our plates and began eating—and laughing as some of our colleagues struggled with the chopsticks.

Finally David stood to speak. "Jan, I have informed your old team about your new role. That's why we're celebrating your return with Chinese food today. Everyone understands that we intend to be more involved in China and around the world. Thanks for being the catalyst who has led us to understand the potential to tap into a more global audience. Now Mark and the team have a presentation for you."

Mark stood next. "Thank you, David," he said. "And yes, we do have something to present to you, Jan. We have read your stories, looked at the pictures of the orphans that you sent, and watched the video. We read about how urgently the little girl, Xiao Ting, needs to have an operation on her heart, so we all contributed for her surgery. Unfortunately, we came up about $2,800 dollars short of your goal, but we want to give this to you to help with her medical care."

I was overwhelmed. I stood and shook Mark's hand, then took a moment to gather myself before speaking to the whole group. "I am moved by your generosity, all of you! Thanks so much for your willingness to assist someone you have never met—I think that speaks volumes about your character. You will never know how much this will help Xiao Ting and relieve Anne, the woman who leads the special needs orphanage. I am thankful to say that I can donate the remaining amount, so we can consider the fundraising for the surgery over. I can't wait to tell Anne and wire her the money!"

David said, "Oh we're not finished yet, Jan. We have more to tell you." I sat back down, stunned. David continued, "I was going past Mark's office, and I saw the video you sent. Mark told me about the list of needs Anne had given you, and he showed me many of the pictures of the children. I'm a father of three healthy boys, and the video and pictures reminded me how fortunate I am, so I wanted to help. My thoughts turned to how I want our company to be a good citizen in the global community, and I've wanted to make a big splash with our entry into the new neighborhood. So I thought of a way we could help the special needs orphanage while creating some marketing buzz for our company. We are going to buy the van Anne said she wanted. I can't imagine the children standing outside in the rain or snow waiting for a taxi, nor can I tolerate the thought of Anne waiting for a taxi to stop if she has a medical emergency with one of the children, so I feel good about this decision."

My colleagues cheered and whistled at David's announcement. Judging by the looks on everyone's faces, David had managed to keep this a secret.

"I am flabbergasted and overwhelmed by your generosity," I said. "I don't know how on earth I can properly thank you! And I can't imagine how excited Anne will be when I email her and tell her about the funds for the operation and the van."

"Why don't you tell her in person, Jan?"

I looked at David blankly. "Tell her in person?"

"Yes. We need you back in China. All of your articles are wonderfully written, but three in particular that you wrote while you were there resonated with so many of the blog readers that we've decided we must do more reporting on those subjects. Also, Lance suggested that we needn't reinvent the wheel, so he has arranged for you to meet with several acclaimed writers who are already living in China, in hopes that we can recruit them for our online publications. You will have to do some traveling and conduct the interviews, but I'm sure that is satisfactory for you. What do you think of returning to China next week and telling Anne then?"

"Oh my! Of course! Yes, I would love to go back! Thank you so much." I saw that my colleagues were beginning to look at their watches, so I signaled that I needed to go, too: "I guess I'd better get to work," I said. "I have a lot to do before I go." On their way out, several colleagues came up to congratulate me or tell me how pleased they were to help Xiao Ting. Clearly, there was going to be sustained interest in the orphanage and Anne's good work.

Though I was still exhausted and fighting jetlag, I had trouble sleeping that night. I kept replaying the day in my mind and struggling with contradictory feelings: I felt so fortunate to have the promotion, but I also felt overwhelmed with all of my new responsibilities. I wanted to be in the office learning more about the new roles I would play, but I was delighted that the company wanted me to return to China so soon. I wanted to be more hands-on with the new teams than these arrangements would allow me to be, but I was thrilled about being able to do so much for Anne and the children.

The next day, I contacted my friends in China to let them know when I was returning, and Holly agreed to make arrangements for me back in our little city. Anne was very happy to hear about the funding for Xiao Ting's surgery. I didn't tell her about the van because I wanted that to be a surprise. I would see her in just a few days and would tell her then.

16

THE CALL

Since learning about my new position within the company, I had felt like I was behind and trying to get caught up in many areas. On the flight back to China, I tried to capitalize on the uninterrupted time. I reviewed the materials each team leader had provided me, as well as resumes from the people I would interview. I knew I needed to improve my skills and learn more about leadership to properly perform my new responsibilities, so I read two books: *The Secret of Teams* by Mark Miller, and *Leaders Open Doors* by Bill Treasurer. By the time the plane landed, I was ready to sleep soundly during the overnight train ride back to our small city.

As Holly had promised, when I exited the lobby of the train station, I saw a driver holding a sign with my name on it. I had to chuckle because I recognized Holly's handwriting, and Lizzy had sketched and colored one of her famous flowers. Their sign certainly stood out.

The driver took me to a restaurant, and Holly, Lizzy, and Canyon were all there to meet me. I was famished and so grateful that they knew I'd want a good meal and some company as soon as I arrived in town. I told them all about my new position, and as usual they were ready to help. Holly said she had a couple of contacts—one in Beijing and one in Shanghai—who might be good candidates for the team I was building. Lizzy and Canyon each gave me the name of a former student they felt could be a good match for the team as well. Of course, I also told them that my colleagues would be funding Xiao Ting's operation and a new van. My friends were as astounded by my company's generosity toward Anne and the children as I had been.

Holly told me that the refrigerator had been delivered and set up, and that the old one had been removed. Holly had filled the new refrigerator with food for the children, and Anne was very pleased.

Everyone was aware that I would spend most of the next day working and visiting Anne and the children. After we left the restaurant, we stopped to have an ice cream at a KFC, where we laughed and gossiped about all of our colleagues from the campus. My walk from there to the hotel was short, which was wonderful because I was beginning to feel very tired.

When I saw all the smiling faces greeting me at Anne's the next day, I forgot all about my challenges with the new position. I was just hanging out with my little buddies, who accepted me and welcomed me even though I didn't look like them, was much older than them, and couldn't communicate with them. I was thinking that total acceptance like this would be a refreshing way to go through life!

When Anne emerged from her office, I asked her if I could see the new refrigerator.

"Of course! What a fantastic surprise that was, and it's so much nicer than our old refrigerator."

"Wonderful. I'm happy you like it. Did the children get in the way while it was being delivered?"

"They did. You know, the children had only seen that one refrigerator, so they were very interested in the new one. It's very different in size and color. And you arranged a second surprise for us, didn't you? As soon as the old refrigerator was removed,

Holly came with a driver whose car was full of food for us. We had a wonderful day!"

"How is Xiao Ting feeling?"

"Not very well at all. She has fainted two more times since you left, and the doctors say she is getting to a critical stage."

"Man, I'm so sorry to hear that! Have you received the money I wired you for the operation?"

"Yes, and the surgery will take place tomorrow. Xiao Ting is at the hospital already."

"It would have been great to see her, but I know she needs to be prepped for her operation and monitored closely. Who is at the hospital with her?"

"The older lady with the curly hair who helps us is there with her. I wanted her to go because she has a bad back, and if she's at the hospital, she won't need to lift children all day long. Her husband wants her to retire because he's afraid she will have significant back problems in the future, but she refuses to retire because she loves the children so much."

"That's a great story. I know you're happy to have someone like that working with you."

"Yes, and she's very experienced with children, so she can do anything and everything requested of her. Now you and I need to talk about the money you wired to me. There was too much. I thought maybe it was a mistake, but the bank assured me that they had received the correct amount. Do you know what happened?"

"It wasn't a mistake. I have another surprise for you. You won't believe this. My boss saw the video I sent to my colleagues to raise support for the operation for Xiao Ting. He began to ask questions, and one of my colleagues showed him more pictures and told him about the list of needs you had shared with me. My boss is the father of three sons, so he has a soft place in his heart for children. He is also a very wise business leader, and he wants our company to expand globally—beginning in China. He wants the company to be seen as a good new neighbor, so he used his influence to get the company to donate enough money to purchase you and the children the van you need."

Anne's jaw dropped open and her face went blank. She attempted to speak multiple times before she worked out a thank you. "I'm stunned," she finally said. "Nobody has ever given us a gift like that before! Most people can't give away so much money. After the expense of the surgery, we will still have about $25,000 left. Can I spend that on the van?"

"Yes, that is your money for the van. Please consider it a gift from my company to you and the children."

"Oh, I can't wait to go shopping for a van, and then I want it to rain the next day. Then the children will see how nice it is to have our own van because we won't have to stand out in the rain trying to get a taxi."

"Ha, that sounds like a good way to break in the van! I'm sure you and the children will get many years of good service from it. Do you know what kind you want?"

"No, I didn't dream I would have one, so I haven't thought about the specifics. I do know that we will need one with impressive seating capacity."

"I'm sure my company will want some pictures of the van once you've purchased it. You and the children have quite a following there!"

"Oh, you can do more than take pictures. I want you to go with me to buy it."

"I don't know anything about buying a van, but I'll be happy to accompany you for moral support."

"I have a driver's license, but I've never purchased a car. Do you have a car?"

"Yes, I have a car, but I've never purchased a new one, and I would imagine buying a vehicle in China is very different from buying one in the States."

"Sounds like we're both inexperienced with this then. Still, I would like it if you could accompany me . . . will you?"

"Sure. I'd also like to see Xiao Ting before her surgery if that's possible. I'm impressed by how quickly you were able to arrange her operation after you received the money."

"She's in a desperate situation, so when you told me you would try to raise the funds for the operation, I asked the doctor to be prepared. Xiao Ting's surgeon agreed to work her into his schedule as quickly as possible. He said it's very bad for her to faint as often as she had started doing."

"Well, I'm happy he was able to work her in and that my friends at work were so generous."

"I was planning to visit her around the time you arrived here. So let's go downstairs and find a taxi to take us to the hospital."

When we arrived at the hospital, I followed Anne, who knew exactly where to go. It wasn't illuminated as well as most hospitals in the States, but I was impressed by how wide the halls were. You could easily have a gurney rolling by on each side of the hall, with plenty of room for people walking between them.

We entered Xiao Ting's room, and I almost burst into tears because she looked so frail. Her lips and fingers were blue like before, but now she looked almost lifeless lying there on the bed. Her eyes were barely open, and she didn't acknowledge us in any way when we entered. Oxygen tubes were going into her nostrils, and she was motionless. While Anne talked with the older lady from the orphanage, I looked around the room. It was a large room with three other patients, each with one or more caregivers.

Xiao Ting was wearing a pair of pajamas that were like a bunny rabbit costume, complete with two large ears. I stroked her forehead, and she rolled her eyes toward me, but there was no life in them. She looked so pitifully weak. It was breaking my heart to see the little girl who had so recently crawled into my lap and into my heart in this condition.

Anne spoke quietly. "Jan, the doctors say that Xiao Ting's condition is worsening rapidly. They are surprised by how quickly she is losing her strength, so they think she may have developed a new problem—or her old condition may have worsened. The surgical team is being assembled earlier than planned, so hers will be the first operation done tomorrow."

"Is there anything I can do to help? It hurts me to see my little lap buddy so weak."

"You and your friends have already done more than we could have expected by paying for her surgery. Your donation came just in time. I don't know how I would have paid for the procedure otherwise."

Xiao Ting was holding my index finger loosely, and my thumb was resting on the back of her hand. "Does she know she will have an operation?"

"Yes. She knows she doesn't feel well and that the doctors will go inside of her and correct the problem so she will once again have strength and energy. She isn't afraid because she wants to feel better."

"Would you please tell her that I love her, and I want her to get well soon? If she will do that, I will come and play with her again. Would you ask her to squeeze my finger if she would enjoy that?"

Anne spoke in a soft, loving voice to Xiao Ting, and I started thinking about how selfish it was of me to ask Xiao Ting to do something for me. To my surprise, I could feel her little fingers grasping my finger just a little bit more tightly. I stroked the back of her hand with my thumb and gave her a smile.

Anne put her hand on my shoulder. "We should leave now and let her get more rest."

"Anne, I'm sure you're right, and I know you have more children to take care of at the orphanage, but would it be okay if I took Xiao Ting's picture before we leave?"

"Sure. Maybe you can send that picture to me as well as to your friends who paid for her operation. She does look sweet in her bunny pajamas."

With our thoughts on Xiao Ting, we didn't speak much during the short taxi ride back to the orphanage. When we entered the apartment with Anne's key rather than ringing the doorbell, we were able to watch the swarm of children form before they approached the entrance, jumping up and down full of joy and excitement to see Anne and me. The little boy with Duchenne muscular dystrophy was one of the most appreciative. He had a perfect little boy smile, complete with something sticky on his face and a gap where he had recently lost his two front teeth. We had a wonderful time playing with the children until the phone in Anne's office rang. She had a long conversation in Chinese, and I could hear that her voice sounded agitated. When she returned, I could tell she had been crying.

"Anne, what is it? What's wrong?" My thoughts immediately went to Xiao Ting.

"That was my friend from the municipal orphanage. New, large orphanages have been opening around the country, so we were concerned about how this could affect smaller facilities. She just learned that the provinces have been ordered by higher levels of government to remove some of the children from smaller orphanages and place them in the new larger ones."

"Why would they do that? Is it to justify the expense of new buildings or the number of people working at the new orphanages?"

"Maybe a little, but they say it is being done so the children will have a better living environment. Everything in these large orphanages is new and clean, and the facilities aren't crowded, so that will be an improvement for the children."

"Does that mean some children will be removed from the municipal orphanage where your friend works?"

"It means that any orphanage in the country can have children removed."

"Including here?"

"Yes, here as well!" Tears raced down Anne's cheeks as she looked around the room at the children she loved and cared for.

"Surely that can't be done! This is their home!"

"You're right, this is their home, but there's nothing we can do besides hope nobody is taken from here."

"It all seems so arbitrary and uncaring."

"Well, this is one way the Chinese and Americans differ. Chinese people look at the larger general picture and want harmony for everyone, and Americans like to drill down to find solutions on an individual level. An American may be able to find a situation in which a child would be better off staying in the orphanage where they are, but it is hard to argue against the point that having a new, cleaner, and more spacious home is a better option. There are so many orphans that it would require too much time and too many people to know what is best for each individual."

"Okay, I see your point, but do you have any options?"

"While I was in my office, I called a friend who is responsible for all orphanages in an entire province and another friend who works in the department responsible for orphans in Beijing. They both told me this would be happening soon and that it's a 'done deal,' as you would say."

"I wish there were something I could do to help prevent this from happening to you and the children."

"I appreciate your thoughts, but please don't do anything. I mean that! We don't want to draw any attention to ourselves now, especially with you being a foreigner. It isn't good for anyone to question a decision made in Beijing."

"I have been told how important it is for everything to be orderly in Chinese society because that proves the government is doing a good job and that they are in control and on top of things."

"Yes, you understand. Now, from what you told me earlier, I think it's time for me to get you into a taxi and on your way to the train station to meet your friend."

I looked at my watch. "Oh my, I didn't realize how late it had gotten. Let me just walk around and say good-bye to everyone, then put on my shoes and I'll be ready to go."

I hugged many of the children and gave one of the workers a bag of balloons. By the time Anne and I were at the elevator, I had already heard two balloons pop. On the way down to the street, I thanked Anne for help with the taxi. "Please let me know how the surgery goes for Xiao Ting," I said. "I'll be in Beijing tomorrow, and I'll have access to email almost all day."

As the taxi rounded the first curve near the park I saw two police cars going toward the orphanage. Chills went down my spine, and I wondered if they were going to remove some of the children.

17

THE TRAIN

The ride to the train station didn't take long at all, and Canyon was waiting at our assigned meeting place near the entrance. She waved as I approached, then greeted me with a hug.

"Are you ready for your train ride in a sleeper car?" Canyon asked me with excitement.

"Absolutely, and I have a wonderful tour guide to assist me with locating the correct train and car."

"I always liked your sense of adventure!"

"I always liked your assistance, because I wouldn't have been able to do many of the things I've done in China if it weren't for your help! Did your husband mind your being out with me this afternoon?"

"Ha, he is watching basketball on CCTV 5, so he may not even know I'm gone!"

"Well I certainly do appreciate your time and assistance with this train trip."

"I think you'll enjoy it, and hopefully you'll be impressed by it."

As we waited for the boarding time, we joked about the transitions we were both facing in our lives—she as a newlywed and me with my new job. We also talked about when I was almost fired from teaching at the university, and about our trip to her hometown to climb a mountain.

"Why are the people lining up at my gate already? There are still forty-five minutes before the train leaves."

"The time on your ticket is for departure, and it takes some time to board the cars."

"Oh, now I understand. So should we get in line?"

"Yes, we should join your new traveling companions."

"Do you think anyone in my compartment will be able to speak English with me?"

"I wouldn't be surprised if someone can. As China becomes more of a world economic power, more and more people are speaking other languages, especially English."

"That makes sense. Can you tell me what to expect on the train?"

"Well, there will be two bathrooms, one at each end of the car. One will have a Western toilet, and the other will have a 'squatty potty.' The restroom with the Western toilet will have a room beside it with several sinks, and I warn you, when you start pulling into Beijing in the morning, those will be busy spots with people brushing their teeth and washing their faces. You should also know that if you stop in a town along the way, the bathroom doors will be locked so no waste from the restrooms is left on the tracks in the station."

"What else can you tell me?"

"As you walk into your room, there will be four beds: two on the bottom and two on the top. There is an open area separating the two sets of bunk beds, and a small table under a window. Each bed will have a reading lamp and a compartment for holding personal belongings. As soon as you step into your room, you'll notice an open area overhead for your luggage. Once you get settled in, usually there will be some casual conversation, and then people will read, send text messages, or go to sleep."

Canyon asked the ticket-taker if she could accompany me onto the train to help me get settled, and was given permission. We found the correct car and boarded, then Canyon walked me to my compartment. She explained the numbering system so I could tell which bed was mine. Then we walked to each end of the car and she showed me the restrooms and the room with the sinks.

"I must get off the train soon," Canyon said. "So are you comfortable with your arrangements?"

"Yes, this is all I need. Thank you so much."

We returned to my cabin, and Canyon spoke with the other people sharing the compartment with me.

"You will have some nice company on the train," she told me. "The young lady is going to Beijing for a job interview, the young man is in graduate school there, and the other lady is a grandmother going to see her family. The two younger people speak English, but the grandmother doesn't. Okay, I have to leave immediately, but they know to make sure you get off the train in Beijing. Good luck with your trip. It was wonderful to see you!"

"Thanks so much for all your help, and hopefully we can spend more time together soon."

Canyon was already going down the hall as I said good-bye. When I returned to the compartment, I looked at my roommates and smiled. The young lady removed one of her headphone earbuds and told me that she spoke English and would be happy to help me with anything. I thanked her and wished her good luck with her interview. She laughed, blushed a little, and said thank you. The older lady offered candy to everyone, but everyone politely declined. The young man was listening to music or watching a movie on his cell phone, but he was already on the top bunk, so I couldn't be sure. I grabbed my toothbrush, toothpaste, and a bottle of water and went to the room with the sinks. There were a couple of other people there brushing their teeth too, and one of them looked startled to see an American riding in the sleeper car.

When I returned to the cabin, everyone was settling in for the night, and I did the same. The sheets and pillowcase appeared to be very clean, and the comforter was plush and warm. When the grandmother opened our door to the hall, I saw a man walking down the hall wearing only a pair of thermal underwear. I guess he was ready for bed. I turned on my reading lamp because I wanted to review some documents in preparation for the interviews, but I soon realized that I wasn't going to make any headway. My eyelids seemed to weigh a thousand pounds, so I just turned off my light and went to sleep.

I must have been exhausted from my travels because I slept very soundly. The next thing I knew, the sun was coming up and I could see the outline of Beijing in the distance. I grabbed a snack that I had brought with me and tried to open it quietly because my roommates were still asleep. I watched Beijing come closer and closer as the sun became brighter. The entire horizon was a continuous series of tall buildings as far as I could see.

As the people on the train began to wake, I ate another snack and went to the restroom, then to the room with the sinks to brush my teeth. I stood for a while to get another view of our approach to Beijing. By now it appeared as if we were in a valley of tall buildings.

I went back into the sleeper car and saw that a line was forming for the restrooms, so I was thankful I'd already used the facilities. Back in the compartment, everyone was awake and on their cell phones. Soon the young man told me that it was time to leave, and we all collected our belongings and went to the end of the hall to get off in Beijing.

I was grateful that the taxi line outside the train station moved quickly because I was ready for a shower at my hotel. I gave the driver the name and address of my hotel, he nodded knowingly, and away we went.

The hotel was located near the train station and had a wonderful English-speaking staff and an absolutely stunning lobby with an enormous chandelier. The floor and walls appeared to be made of marble with beautiful inlaid designs.

Up in my room, I checked email, did some more work, and showered. Then I went out for lunch. On the way back, I took a look at the conference room the hotel had made available for the interview. They had made impressive arrangements.

The candidate arrived on time (a critical indicator for me), and we went upstairs to the conference room. I had a very good feeling about her. She was an extremely experienced writer but still had the eager enthusiasm of someone just out of school. We discussed the requirements of the job, as well as the challenges of the time difference and of working remotely without a team right down the hall supporting her.

She said that she was comfortable with the job description and with the idea of not having a team nearby, so we reviewed some of her recent work. I was surprised when she complimented my articles about China that the company had posted online. She was impressed with my understanding of the Chinese perspective on various issues. I explained that I had surrounded myself with wise counselors who had taught me most of what I knew about China.

As the interview concluded, I gave her the standard line about having other candidates to consider, and I promised that she would hear from me again. I gave her my business card with both hands, and she smiled and said she knew from my writing that I was picking up on Chinese culture, and that using two hands to give her something as small as a business card proved it.

18

WHIRLWIND

After the interview, I rushed back to my room to call Anne and check on Xiao Ting. Anne sounded exhausted. "Thanks for checking, Jan. The surgeons said that the damage was more severe than expected, so the procedure took longer to complete than they thought it would. She's still asleep, but the doctors feel confident that the problems have been resolved. They are very concerned about how long she was under anesthesia, and they don't like how small and weak she was when the surgery was performed. They wish they could have waited for her to be larger and stronger, but of course her condition made that impossible."

"It's good to hear that the doctors think they've resolved all the issues. Did they say when she would wake up?"

"That's a good question, but nobody knows when she'll wake up, not even the surgeon or the doctor who administered the anesthesia."

"That makes me nervous! Is there anything I can do for you or the children?"

"No, there's nothing that can be done, but thanks for offering."

"Okay. I'll be working in Beijing for the rest of today, and tomorrow I'll fly to Shanghai for another interview. When Xiao Ting wakes up or when you have some news, please let me know."

"I will. Hopefully I'll have some good news for you soon!"

I spent the rest of the day preparing for the interview in Shanghai and working on the articles David wanted completed, but my mind kept drifting to Xiao Ting and to Anne and her concerns about the children being removed. I also emailed the group at work about Xiao Ting's surgery because I knew they wanted an update.

The next morning I was up before dawn for my trip to Shanghai. The sun was just starting to come up as the flight took off, and it was beautiful to watch it from the air. As we approached Shanghai, I was amazed by the city's enormous size. Shanghai is larger than Beijing, and it's considered the economic capital of China. The buildings are more modern than those in Beijing, the climate is warmer, and the air is clearer.

The clerks at the front desk of my hotel in Shanghai spoke English well and were very polite. My room was exceptionally clean and modern, and I was glad to see a couple of free bottles of water because I hate paying airport prices for bottled water. The conference room I had reserved was also very clean and had ultramodern furniture.

I was all set for the interview, so I went back to my room to do some work. I opened an email from Mark that was flagged as urgent. He informed me that he needed to speak with me via Skype or phone within the next day or two. I found it interesting that he used the word *needed* instead of *wanted* and that he said he would prefer a call, which told me he wanted a little privacy. Mark chooses his words carefully, so I suspected that there was a problem back at work that couldn't be easily resolved. With the time difference between China and the States, it wasn't a good time to call, so I responded to other emails until it was time for the interview.

Lance and his team had done a fantastic job finding these candidates. Both of them were very well educated and highly experienced with the type of work we would be requiring them to perform. One disadvantage today's interviewee faced, though, was that the competing candidate in Beijing was amazing. I had connected with her immediately. I knew I was looking for competence, character, and chemistry with each candidate, but because Lance and his team were prescreening the candidates and doing background checks, I was focusing more on chemistry.

Today's interviewee was very professional, and he presented himself well, but he seemed overly proud of himself and his accomplishments. I was concerned about how his personality would be received by our team. By the end of the interview, I was convinced he had all of the capabilities to perform the job, but my gut was telling me to keep looking. I thanked him for his time and informed him that I was looking at many candidates and would be in touch with him soon.

I went back to my room and changed into some comfortable walking shoes, because Canyon had told me about an area of Shanghai called the Bund, which she said I had to visit. I grabbed my travel guide, did some quick research, and headed out. The front desk staff told me that the Bund was about a twenty-minute walk away, and they gave me a street map. I would be careful to look for landmarks and keep an eye on the map.

As I was walking, I decided to call Anne to check on Xiao Ting. She had discouraging news. The doctors had said that Xiao Ting was very weak, and she still hadn't woken up from the surgery."

"Wow," I said. "That's a long time for her to be asleep. Are the doctors worried about it?"

"Yes, they are very concerned, and they still have her connected to ventilator. I'm worried about her strength. I don't know how to explain it, but she just doesn't look good to me. I have seen many children go through operations before, and they all looked better afterward than Xiao Ting does now."

"What have the doctors said about her staying on the ventilator?"

"The short story is they don't know when she will improve enough to be removed from the ventilator, and they have many other machines monitoring her breathing, pulse, temperature, and who knows what else."

"I'm sorry she isn't responding more quickly. I'll continue to check in with you about her condition. Is there anything I can do for you or for the children?"

"Yes, I was serious when I said I wanted you to go with me to buy the van. The sooner the better because I'm spending lots of money going back and forth to the hospital every day in taxis."

"Okay, let me think through my schedule and travel plans, and I'll let you know when I can come."

"That sounds good to me. Thank you for your willingness to help."

"Anne, I do so little compared to you, so I should be the one thanking you for the love and nurturing you give the children."

"Ha, no need to thank me. I'm just doing what is on my heart to do. Please stay in touch and let me know when you can come."

"Okay, I will do that. It may be sometime tomorrow before I determine my plans. Good-bye."

I continued walking and looking at my map, but my thoughts were on Xiao Ting and I was wondering what was on Mark's mind. When I arrived at the area on my map labeled as the Bund, I was surprised to see many older structures built in a European architectural style. My guidebook informed me that Shanghai had long been an international city with a significant European presence. Running near the European buildings was the wide Huangpu River, and I saw several barges traveling up and down it. Across the river I saw a very tall building with a unique shape. I knew at once that it was the Pearl TV tower, which my students had told me about. The building was tall and thin, with a couple of large round areas shaped like pearls. My map said there was a train tunnel that went under the river, but I didn't want to take the time to find it or use it.

Canyon had also told me about Nanjing Street, which has appeared in many movies because it has so many shops with bright, multicolored neon lights. It wasn't quite dark yet, and I wanted to see the street at night, so I went to a Western-style restaurant for dinner. The food was very good, and the waitress spoke English well enough to easily tell me the quickest way to get to Nanjing Street. When I got there, I saw that the street was as impressive as Canyon had promised. No cars were allowed on it, and it was filled with pedestrians as far as I could see. Upscale stores and people loaded down with shopping bags lined both sides of the street. Not every establishment was upscale, though. I saw a McDonald's with a walk-up window where you could only get a beverage or ice cream. If you wanted a meal, you had to go inside.

Finally I made my way back to the hotel. It was a good thing I had my map or I would have gotten lost several times. It would have been very embarrassing to get in a taxi and ask the driver to take me just two blocks.

When I returned to my room, I called Mark and learned about a new problem at work. Joey, one of the seven team leaders, was disgruntled because he had worked for the company longer than I had, and he felt that he should have been given the promotion instead of me. Unfortunately, Joey's dissatisfaction was influencing others, which isn't good for employee morale, so I needed to meet with him soon to patch things over. I had met with all of the team leaders individually before this trip to China, and he had appeared to be fine with reporting to me at the time. Now I felt torn between wanting to help Anne and see Xiao Ting again and needing to get back to the office quickly to address the issue with Joey.

I realized that if I planned carefully, I could do both. I went to the concierge's desk and asked the staff there if they knew of any way I could travel back to Anne's city that night. One woman pulled out a large laminated sheet of paper with a spreadsheet on it. She said that there were no flights that evening and no train service until the next day. Then she said, "If your desire is to travel, may I suggest Xi'an, Qingdao, or perhaps Hainan?"

"Oh, this isn't for a vacation, but thanks for the suggestion." Then the other concierge, who was looking at a computer screen, said, "There is a sleeper bus leaving in two hours from the nearest bus station, but that is the only one for tonight."

"Do you think I can get there in time for the bus? And if I can, could you write in Chinese what I would need to show someone to get a ticket?"

"Yes, you can get there in time. I'll tell the front desk to get your paperwork ready for your checkout. Also, I'll ask the bellman to hold a taxi for you, and I'll tell him which bus station the driver needs to take you to."

"This is happening so quickly. I'll go up and pack right now and meet the bellman downstairs."

"Yes, that will work."

"You have been a huge help to me. Thank you so very much!"

"It's my pleasure to serve you, and hopefully you'll have a good trip."

With that, I hurried back to my room to pack. By the time I returned to the front desk, my paperwork had already been printed, and the bellman and the concierge were waiting for me.

"We have a taxi ready for you," the bellman said, "and we have written down the correct bus station for the driver. Also, we have written down the ticket request for you to give the teller. The tellers will all be working inside a booth with an all-glass front. Just slide your paper to them to receive your ticket. If you give the teller five hundred yuan, they will give you the correct change. It will be easy for you."

"Thanks so much. I couldn't have done this without your help!"

"It is my pleasure. You should leave now to catch your bus."

The old Jan would never have trusted so many people she didn't know in such a short period of time for something as critical as her travel plans!

19

THE BUS

The taxi driver drove quickly and aggressively to the bus station, so I imagine that the bellman had told him to hurry. He even got into a slight argument with the parking lot attendant at the bus station so he could drop me off at the entrance instead of making me walk through a huge parking lot. Because he did all of that for me, I gave him a fifty yuan bill to cover a thirty-eight yuan charge, and I left before he could hand me any change.

As the bellman had told me, it was easy to find the ticket-purchasing area. I went to an open window and slid the note the bellman had written for me to a woman behind the glass enclosure. She read the note, pointed to the clock, and slid me the ticket. I gave her the amount of money the bellman said to give her, and she gave me some change. I was thinking about how easy the process had been, but then things changed.

The teller started speaking to me in Chinese extremely quickly, and I became confused. I withdrew a step from the window to see if anyone was around who might be able to help me, but there was nobody. I gave the teller the universal shoulder shrug, and three people in the ticket office started laughing. A couple of them pointed which way I should go, so I put the change in my pocket, nodded my thanks, and walked away in the direction they had indicated.

I walked down a dark hallway with many vendors of various types lining the walls. The hallway then opened into a large lobby area with another long hallway off of it. This hallway had glass walls through which I could see all of the buses with people boarding, and workers putting luggage on top of some of the buses.

I looked at my ticket and focused on the numbers, trying to find my gate number. I could tell which number was the departure time, and there was another number in dark large print which I assumed was my gate number. I walked down the glass-walled hallway until I found that gate number and showed my ticket to a man at the door. He nodded his head yes, so I figured I was at the right gate. Once I knew I had found my bus, I called Anne to let her know that if she was available the next morning, I would come by her apartment to go with her to purchase a van.

"Hello Anne, this is Jan. I hope I'm not calling you too late."

"No, it isn't too late, but it happened!"

"Anne, what happened? Is Xiao Ting okay?"

"The officials came and removed seven children from here and put them in the new large orphanage. There was nothing I could do because they had all of the paperwork with the official chop, or 'seal' as you call it, so they are gone. Seven of my children are gone!"

"Anne, I am so sorry to hear that! Is there nothing you can do?"

"No, there is nothing that can be done. Don't you remember? You were here when my friend from the municipal orphanage called and told me what was going to happen, and I contacted more people who would know about the situation. They all said that nothing could be done at the local level to alter a decision that had been made so high up in our country's leadership structure."

"Yes, I do remember, but I guess in my heart I didn't believe it could really happen. I'm so sorry for you and the children. Is there anything I can do to help?"

"I must be strong for the children because they were frightened, but there is nothing you can do to assist with this situation. If you can help me select the van, that would be wonderful. Maybe it will take the children's minds off what has happened to their brothers and sisters."

"Then that is what we'll do. Try to get some rest. I'm on the sleeper bus from Shanghai on the way to help you purchase the van tomorrow morning."

"That's great, and I'm excited about getting the van, but you can't be on a sleeper bus."

"Why can't I be on a sleeper bus? Someone at the hotel wrote it in Chinese, and the person selling the tickets gave me the ticket."

"Two days ago a sleeper bus was in a very bad accident, and there was a fire on the bus. Several people were trapped inside and couldn't get out, so they died in the wreck and fire. Now there's a mandatory inspection of all sleeper buses that go through our province, and none of them can be used until they have all passed the inspection so everyone can know the buses are safe. I think you will be on a normal bus, one with seats and not beds."

"You know, the lady who sold me the ticket was trying to tell me something, but I didn't understand her, so maybe that was what she attempted to communicate to me. I'm sorry to hear about the wreck; that must have been horrible."

"Yes, it was terrible, but don't worry. You will be okay on the bus you are on."

"That's good to know! Anyway, I'm not certain about what time I will get to your apartment, but I will come directly there from the bus station."

"Okay. I look forward to seeing you. Try to sleep on the trip."

"Anne, take care of the kids and yourself. And again, I am so sorry about the children being removed from your care. I'll see you in the morning. Good night to you and the children."

I joined the line that was forming at the door to our gate. I could tell by the line that the bus would be full, but I didn't realize how full. When I handed my ticket to the woman at the top of the bus stairs, she took one step down the aisle and pointed to the seat number over a first-row seat, and then she pointed to a corresponding number on my ticket. That was my seat, and I was horrified about it. Instead of having a row to myself so I could stretch out and get some sleep, I would be sharing the row with a woman holding a child who looked to be about seven years old. The child was way too large to be considered a lap child, but maybe the woman was just trying to save some money.

I looked toward the back of the bus to see if I had other options, but the bus was full. And not only was I sharing the row with a third person, there was a metal counter directly in front of our seats that held a container of water for all passengers. So not only could I not stretch out, but interruptions from people coming to get water would occur all night long. A few people came to the front of the bus to fill their tea jars with water just as the bus started backing up, so people were stumbling and nearly falling on top of me already. My mood worsened even further when a Kung Fu movie started and I saw that the TV was mounted right in front of me and blaring at full volume!

20

NEGOTIATIONS

The woman and her child in the seat next to me both went to sleep quickly, and I tried to do the same but wasn't successful. I knocked out a couple of hours of work on my laptop before the battery ran low, and then I leaned back in my seat and tried to get some rest. But my mind kept racing. Only a few days ago I was on an emotional high with having a wonderful new job, being part of the group that provided for the surgery for Xiao Ting, and obtaining funds for a van for Anne and the children. But now, Xiao Ting was weak and on a ventilator, seven children had been removed from Anne's home, and I had a troublemaker on one of my teams at work. On top of that, the candidate I had gone to Shanghai to interview didn't seem like a good fit with our team. It was a good thing that I had an aisle seat because otherwise I would have become very claustrophobic. I needed help, and I didn't know where to turn!

Feeling grungy and sorry for myself, I sent Lizzy a text message telling her that I was on the night-time bus and asking if I could run by her apartment for a shower in the morning when the bus got in. She replied that she would leave a key under the mat for me but wouldn't be there because she had a meeting. My next text was to Anne to offer a few words that I hoped would be comforting to her and telling her that I would be a little later than we initially thought. With thoughts of a hot shower in my mind, I was finally able to slip into a shallow, frequently interrupted sleep.

I awoke with a jolt hours later when our bus ran over the curb while pulling into the station. Thankfully because of my first-row seat, I was the first one off the bus. Luckily I still had my taxi directions for the town with me. Jumping into a taxi, I pointed at the paper to show the driver where I wanted to go, and he nodded. I slept again in the taxi until the big bump at the entrance to the campus awakened me.

To thank Lizzy for allowing me to shower at her apartment, I left her some American cookies that I thought she would like. Her hot water heater was mounted on the wall, and it had a far greater capacity than the one I had when I lived on campus, so I enjoyed a long, hot shower. I then wrapped myself in one of Lizzy's soft, fluffy towels. I couldn't understand how she got her towels so soft and fluffy since we all hung our clothes to dry. I got dressed and immediately went to Anne's.

This time when a worker opened the door at Anne's, the children initially seemed afraid. However, the moment they recognized me they came running and wanted me to pick them up and hold them. I knew their sadness from having their playmates removed so suddenly and sat on the floor and tried to engage with as many of them as I could. Maybe it was all in my mind, but the orphanage had a different, almost eerie feel to it.

Anne entered the room looking tired and sad. "Are you ready to go shopping for the van?" she asked.

"Sure. Would it be okay if I left my backpack here?"

"Yes, that will be fine, but let me go lock it in my office so the children won't bother it."

As we exited the building, Anne asked, "Do you have much room in your fanny pack?"

"Not too much because I have my camera in there. Why do you ask?"

"Well, I have $25,000 cash in this bag, and I wanted to see if it would fit in your fanny pack so it would be safer."

"Anne, why do you have all of that cash with you?"

"Well, I want to pay cash for the van."

"Okay, I will make room for the cash." Getting all that money into my fanny pack and zipping it closed turned out to be a feat of engineering.

As we entered the taxi, Anne told the driver where to go. She then asked me, "Do you have your driver's license with you?"

"Yes, but why do you want to know about my driver's license?"

"Because I'm hoping you can drive the new van back to my apartment. I haven't driven in two years, so my confidence isn't very high."

"But my driver's license is for America, not China. I can't legally drive here."

"No, I think you're wrong. I think an American driver's license is just as good as an international driver's license."

"Anne, we'd better be absolutely certain. If there was an accident and my driver's license wasn't valid in China, I would be in lots of trouble."

"Wait a minute, I will ask the driver." Anne and the taxi driver had a conversation about my driver's license. She then turned to me and said, "The driver agrees with me. He thinks an American driver's license is the same as an international driver's license, so you can drive the van home for me."

"Okay, I'll do it," I said, but I was still worried.

We turned onto a street with multiple car dealerships, and Anne announced that she'd been doing some research. "I think I know which company's van I want. I told the driver to take us there first."

We walked around the dealership and looked a several models of vans, and Anne told me which one she liked the best. It came as no surprise to me because she had been hovering around it like a bird of prey waiting to swoop in to get its prize.

"Anne, this vehicle has a clutch. Do you know how to drive a standard transmission?"

"It's been a long time since I have driven with a clutch, but I have done it before."

"Are you sure you want a van with a standard—rather than an automatic—transmission?"

"Yes, that's what I want because it will save me gas money. Okay, I see what is available here and the prices. Let's go and look at another dealership."

As soon as we got halfway to the second dealership, it started raining. Unfortunately, the rain seemed to stop during our visit to each dealership and return while we walked to the next one. After we had visited all of the dealerships on the street, Anne invited me to have lunch with her while we discussed our options.

"So tell me," I asked when we were seated at our table, "which van is your favorite one now that you have had a chance to see so many?"

"I still like the black one at the first dealership we went to, because it has lots of room for the children."

"Yes, I remember that one. It had a clutch, right?"

"That's the one. But I also want a DVD player in it for the children, so we'll have to ask about that."

"Great idea. I'm sure the children will love it. Have you thought about getting some car seats?"

"No, I don't want any car seats. I'm not even sure you can buy them in our city. They are not used very commonly in China, though I think the big cities are starting to sell more of them."

"But Anne, they will help protect the small children if there is a wreck."

"The van is big, so it's easy for people to see it and nobody will hit us."

"Anne, I appreciate your optimism, but if we can negotiate a good price maybe you will have some money left over for car seats, gas, insurance, and maintenance."

"Yes, I do want to have money left over for such things. That's why I want you to negotiate the price for me—since you have bought a vehicle before."

"I'm sure you've negotiated more prices than me because it's so commonly done in China. Maybe you would get a better deal than me!"

"No, I want you to think it through for me and do the talking. I'll translate for you."

"Okay. If that's how you want to do it, that's what we'll do. Have you heard anything about Xiao Ting's condition today?"

"She hasn't changed. She's still connected to the ventilator."

"Man, I sincerely wish she would wake up and crawl up into my lap again so we could look at a book together."

"Yes, that would be nice, but the doctors say they don't know when she will be strong enough to breathe on her own."

"I hope you will keep me updated on her condition—even after I have returned to the States."

"Yes, I will."

"I can't tell you how badly I feel about her weakness because my friends and I paid for the surgery. If she had never had the operation, she might have been better off than she is now."

"Please don't blame yourself. You and your friends were doing a wonderful and generous thing. That would be like me blaming myself because children were just removed from my care. I didn't do anything wrong, but they were removed anyway."

"I see your point, so I'll try not to beat myself up too much about it. Have you heard anything about the children who were sent to the large new orphanage?"

"No, and I don't expect to hear from anyone unless someone has a question about a health concern for one of the children."

"This process baffles me. I would call it a catastrophic failure to do what is best for the children."

"I agree, but that is how things are done in China, and some of our ways are hard for a foreigner to understand."

"You've told me before that you have traveled to other provinces to pick up children. Do you notice any differences between the orphanages you've visited?"

"Yes, I've seen a huge difference. I've seen orphanages that were extremely impressive, and I've seen some that made you worry about the children immediately."

"For example?"

"I've seen some orphanages that were housed in immaculate new buildings. They had a large enough staff that each worker only takes care of a few children. The closest ones like that are in Beijing."

"How can they afford such facilities and such a high level of staffing?"

"The really impressive orphanages seem to have some type of financial support that others don't have. These orphanages are supported by businesses or foreigners. In some cases, they are supported by foreign businesses. The nicest ones can even afford to have teachers and therapists come in daily."

"What are orphanages like at the other end of the spectrum?"

"Horrible. So horrible I want to cry just thinking about them. Let's change the subject back to buying the van. Are you ready to negotiate a great deal?"

"Sure. This may be an educational experience of a lifetime for me, and I'm excited to see what happens."

As Anne and I walked back to the first dealership, we discussed all of the options she wanted on the van and our strategy for negotiating a better price. I remembered that the salesperson we had spoken to was a young, very tall woman, and I wanted to find her again.

When we entered the dealership, I saw the woman in the back and waved to her. She came toward the front of the showroom, and I asked Anne to tell her that we wanted to discuss some options for the black van and see what it would cost. She welcomed us to an area with a desk and chairs, and she pulled out some paperwork. She and Anne spoke for a few moments, and Anne told me she had given the sales lady the list of options she wanted. The lady took out a calculator and began adding up the total cost of the van with all of the options. We didn't have a language barrier now because numbers were something we could all understand. The salesperson slid the document over to Anne, who slid it over to me, and I saw that we were at almost $30,000 US dollars. I told Anne that we would have to get the price reduced, and she emphatically agreed.

I told Anne to tell the salesperson that we would pay $17,000 for the van with the options. Anne translated that for me. The woman wrote down our offer and carried it over to the sales manager. She came back and said that the sales manager had told her we were not even close to a suitable price.

I suggested to Anne that she tell the woman that the van was going to be for orphans, hoping that she and the sales manager would be sensitive to our cause. Then I asked Anne to up our offer by $500. When the woman returned this time, she reported that the sales manager had come down a few thousand dollars, but we still couldn't afford the price.

I told Anne to tell the salesperson that there were many vans for sale on this street, and we knew where to find ones that cost less than this one. Also, because the sales manager thought this van was worth so much money, I wanted Anne to test drive it.

Anne and the salesperson talked some more. Anne then told me that in China you are not allowed to test drive a vehicle. She told me the salesperson had said, "If it's broken then we can't sell it."

I realized that our insistence on test driving could be leverage for us in negotiating the price, so I told Anne to ask the salesperson how she could expect us to spend that much money on something if we don't know whether it works or not.

Again Anne translated my thoughts to our salesperson, who leaned back in her chair and looked upward as if she were deep in thought. She excused herself and went to see the sales manager again. This time when she returned, she had a significantly better price. Also, she told us that the DVD player Anne wanted was only installed at the factory and that their service department couldn't do the installation.

The poor salesperson was wearing out the carpet between her cubicle and the sales manager's office as we cycled through more offers and counteroffers until we settled on a final price of $20,000, which left enough for insurance, gas, and maintenance. Anne told me, "The sales manager has agreed to the price, which doesn't include the DVD player, but the salesperson has agreed to pay for the DVD player herself because it's for the children."

"Wonderful, and I think this is a great deal! Now you have money left over for the insurance and other things. Please tell the salesperson thanks for her generous offer to provide the DVD player for the children." I was relieved that the DVD player would need to be installed at the factory because I definitely didn't want to drive the new van back to Anne's home.

While we waited for the paperwork, I asked Anne whether she had called the insurance company to arrange for insurance. "No," she answered. "It wouldn't do any good to call them because you must drive the vehicle you want to insure to their office. Then you can get insurance."

"So are you telling me that the insurance companies want you to drive an uninsured vehicle to their office to get it insured?"

"Yes, that is the process we use here."

"But what if you are in an accident on the way to the insurance office?"

"Well, you must drive very carefully to the insurance office!" We both started laughing at how pointless the practice was. Anne said, "You were pretty good at negotiating the price for the van. Many foreigners don't like to negotiate, so I was impressed with your determination."

"Like our salesperson, I was doing it for your precious children!"

21

CONFRONTATION

Anne took a taxi home and I took one to Holly's, where she had a driver waiting for me. Holly and I had a quick conversation, and she then told me that I should get going if I was going to make my flight. It would be a long drive back to Beijing, where I would catch my flight back to the States, but fortunately the driver had already planned a trip there to visit a family member. With thoughts of Xiao Ting, the removal of Anne's children, and the problem at work with Joey all jostling for the pole position in my mind, I got as comfortable as I could in the back seat of the driver's car. I soon fell into a much-needed deep sleep. The next thing I knew, we were at the airport.

Only a few people were ahead of me at the check-in counter, so I hoped the flight wouldn't be very crowded. Sure enough, as the plane was preparing to depart, several people began changing seats to find ones where they could have a little more room to stretch out and get some sleep. Fortunately I had a couple of seats all to myself, and I intended to get as much sleep as possible. For a while my mind raced with worry, but soon enough exhaustion caught up with me again, and I slept until we were almost ready to land back in the States.

Lance agreed to meet me early on my first day back in the office. We had a good conversation about the people I had interviewed in China, and I learned that he and his team had identified additional qualified candidates. As for Joey, Lance said that if Joey insisted he wasn't going to work for me, it was clearly insubordination and grounds for termination. He said Joey's undermining my authority and saying negative things about David's decisions were also grounds for dismissal. If I decided I wanted to fire him, Lance and Human Resources would back my decision completely.

Later that morning, while waiting for my meeting with Joey, I reviewed the progress of the seven teams I managed. Each of the teams was making good progress except for Joey's, which had fallen significantly behind schedule. When Joey walked into my office, my heart began to race. I wanted desperately for this conversation to go well, and I had rehearsed what I wanted to say a million times in my mind, but now I wasn't sure I would remember everything I had planned to say.

I took a deep breath and dived right in. "Joey, there are two things I want to discuss with you this morning. One is your team's performance, and the other is your performance. If I understand the timeline of your team's project, it appears that you're significantly behind schedule. What is most alarming to me is how quickly this tardiness has developed. Can you make me aware of what has caused this problem and what measures have been implemented to get the team back on track?"

"Well," Joey answered, "we've had multiple problems. Our computers are too slow for us to get our work done in a timely manner, and my team is incompetent."

"Joey, stop right there and think about what you're saying and to whom you're saying it. I know what computers your team uses because they are the same systems my old team used, and we never had a capacity or speed problem. Also, your team is literally an award-winning team. So is there anything else going on that you want to discuss?"

"No. I just can't work with those people any longer!"

"I am sorry to hear that, and judging by the inflection of your voice, I can tell you truly mean it." After some digging, I learned that Joey's dissatisfaction about David's decision to promote me wasn't the core problem. Rather, Joey didn't have passion about his work any longer because he wanted to work with the graphic design department. He had gone to night classes and achieved many certifications. So Joey was now very qualified for that type of work, and he was ready to switch gears. Joey and I struck a deal: if he got his team back on track and their project was completed on time and at a high level of quality, I would do all I could do to get him a job in the graphic design department. Joey understood that I had set some measurable short-term goals for him. He knew that if he failed to meet them, my offer to assist him in securing a new position in graphic design would be withdrawn, and his career at our company would be at risk.

Because it wasn't too late in China, I called Anne to check on Xiao Ting's condition. I was hopeful that with one big problem moving in the right direction, perhaps Anne would have additional good news.

"Ni hao," Anne greeted me over the phone.

"Hey Anne, this is Jan. How are you doing today?"

"Not very good."

"Oh no! What's wrong? Is Xiao Ting okay?"

"No, she's not doing well at all. Today the doctors took her off the ventilator, and she didn't respond well. She is so weak that she couldn't breathe on her own for five minutes. If the doctors had not reconnected her to the ventilator, she would have died. In fact, they told me that she may not live through the night!"

"Oh my gosh, that's horrible news! Can we do something to help her? Does she need to go to another hospital or get another doctor?"

"No, she is much too weak to travel or be moved, so all we can do is hope she can survive until she grows stronger."

"Oh dear. And again, I feel guilty because our donation paid for the surgery that caused her to be so weak."

"Jan, you mustn't put yourself through that; you were trying to help. She was so weak that she was fainting. You and your friends gave her a significantly better chance to thrive than I could have given her."

"I'm so sorry for you, because I know it makes it harder for you to have someone in the hospital with Xiao Ting twenty-four hours a day and still take care of all of the other children. Please know that my heart is with you and the children, even if my body isn't."

"Thank you, and it is wonderful for me to know how much you care because I don't get much encouragement. You know, most people don't want to see special needs children. Sometimes I feel as if I'm on an island all by myself."

"I think I kind of understand. Growing up here in the States as an orphan, I was one of the children who wasn't invited to spend the night at friends' houses and go to parties and things like that. So yes, I too have often felt like I was all alone on an island. I need to get back to work now, but please let me know if there are any changes, Anne, and I will stay in touch with you."

I had so wanted to hear good news about Xiao Ting and her health, but instead I felt I could potentially be playing a role in her death. I was on an emotional roller coaster and didn't know where to turn for help. I began to feel like I was back on the island Anne and I were talking about.

22

IT COULD GET WORSE

Holly called shortly after I hung up the phone with Anne. "I just spoke to Anne," I told her, "and she gave me an update on Xiao Ting's condition, so I guess you know how badly she's doing."

"Yes, I know. Lizzy and I have been trying to help when we can. Xiao Ting looks frightfully pale to me, but I know she has to be improving each day, even if we can't measure her progress."

"That's encouraging to hear. Hopefully you're right. If anything happened to her, I don't know what I would do!"

"I'm calling you to tell you about something else. Xinhua, the official Chinese news agency, is reporting that six children have perished in a fire at an independent orphanage in the center of the country."

"Oh my goodness, that's horrible! What will happen to the other children since their orphanage burned?"

"There is a municipal orphanage nearby, so they will receive the children, but that isn't why I am telling you this. Since you're not Chinese, you may not understand the implications. When a catastrophic situation like this occurs, the government will do something to restore order and ensure everyone that steps are being taken to resolve the issue and prevent a similar situation from occurring elsewhere. So, for example, if a boat sinks and people are injured or drown, the government may want to do something like make all boats have an escape raft, carry life vests, and pass an inspection."

"I think I understand. So Anne may need to buy fire extinguishers or have a sprinkler system installed in the orphanage."

"Exactly. You see the logic, don't you?"

"Yes, the government wants to assure the public that they are taking reasonable steps to ensure safety for everyone. That makes perfectly good sense to me."

"Okay then. I know you're busy at work, so I'll leave you alone, but I did want you to know about that horrible orphanage fire."

"Thanks so much, Holly, and please let me know if anything develops from the fire that affects Anne and the children. Poor Anne doesn't need anything else to worry about!"

My day was a blur as I tried to assist the teams under me and recruit for the international team I was building. Additionally, I worked with Human Resources to prepare to interview more candidates and to make a job offer to the woman I interviewed in Beijing. I worked late, but decided to leave the office before my focus decreased further due to exhaustion from the day's happenings.

At home I prepared a light meal and was finally relaxing in front of the TV when my phone rang.

"Hello."

"Hey, Jan, this is Lizzy. Hopefully I didn't catch you at a bad time."

"No, I just got home from the office, so I made a little something to eat and started watching TV. How is Xiao Ting?"

"Xiao Ting is weak—so unbelievably weak. The doctors tried again to remove her from the ventilator, but she couldn't breathe on her own. They had to reconnect the ventilator immediately. After that failed attempt, the doctors said they don't think she will survive."

"Oh, that's devastating. I so wish there were something we could do."

"We all feel the same, but Xiao Ting isn't why I called you. I wanted to give you further information about the fire and the government's response. To ensure the safety of children in independent orphanages, government officials will inspect each independent orphanage to confirm that certain levels of care and safety are provided. Additionally, each province has the authority to remove any child who is from their province but is in an independent orphanage in another province, and transfer that child to a municipal orphanage in the child's home province."

"But what about taking a child away from their home—is that the best thing for them? I know how difficult bouncing from one home to another can be, because that happened to me as an orphan. Are any of Anne's children from other provinces?"

"Yes. She currently has about fifteen children from other provinces."

"So you are telling me that potentially fifteen children could be removed and placed in municipal orphanages in other provinces?"

"Yes, that is the situation; and just like with the children being relocated to the new large municipal orphanages, there is nothing that can be done. When the government makes a quick decision and lays out such an aggressive plan, there is absolutely no way to avoid the consequences."

"When will the inspections and removals begin?"

"They have already started in the province where the fire occurred, and I'm sure other provinces will follow quickly. I just wanted you to know what's going on, and I'm sorry to have bad news to report."

"I just can't imagine some of the children we have grown so close to being removed. Ugh! I hate not being able to control things like this. I wish there were some way we could protect our little friends."

"Your thoughts are nice, but again, there is nothing you or anyone else can do to stop this decision."

"Well, thanks for calling, and please let me know what happens next. If you talk to Anne, please give her my best."

Wow, just when I thought things couldn't get any worse! I felt so sorry for Anne. Xiao Ting was near death, and now there was the possibility of officials coming in to remove more children from her home, when her help was stretched to its limits.

23

PLEASE DON'T TAKE MY CHILDREN

All weekend long I wondered what Joey would have to say on Monday morning. My thoughts were also on the situation at Anne's. I kept hoping someone would call and say Xiao Ting was getting better, but instead she remained on the ventilator. I was thankful, though, that she was still with us. Holly told me that not only were officials going into independent orphanages around the country to inspect them, but they were interviewing people working at the orphanages and even bringing the police with them. I could only imagine how scary it would be for children to be removed and placed in a new environment—and likewise how scary it would be for the children who were allowed to stay. Would they be afraid that the officials would come back and remove them too? I needed some peace about this situation but had no idea where to find it.

On Monday morning, I was at work early to get my week started. David had left a handwritten note on my desk saying he was pleased with the work I did in China, and there might be more. I should keep my bags packed. I was relieved that he was pleased—that was one concern off my plate. Hoping that David's note was the beginning of a trend of good news, I decided to call Anne before it got too late for her to take a call.

"Ni hao."

"Hello, Anne. This is Jan, checking in to see how you and the children are doing today."

"No change for Xiao Ting," Anne said. "She is still very weak. The doctors said they may try to take her off the ventilator again in a few days, but they are very nervous when she doesn't breathe on her own, and so am I."

"Yeah, I am too. How is the situation with children being removed from independent orphanages?"

"Not good. The inspections are taking place all around the country, and many children have been removed and returned to their home provinces."

"Do you think they will come to your orphanage?"

"Yes, they will go to every orphanage like mine, but we don't know when. I think it will be very soon, because my friend who works in Beijing called me and told me to expect them any day."

"Anne, I hope the inspection turns out well for you and the children! Well, I know you probably have children to put to bed, so I'll let you go. Please know that my thoughts are with you."

Because Mark's team had done so much to make the surgery for Xiao Ting a reality, I had been keeping them updated on her progress. It was amazing to me how often someone would ask me in the hall about Xiao Ting's status, and it was encouraging to have such a good group of people pulling for her. On Monday afternoon, Mark brought me an additional contribution from his team for Xiao Ting's ongoing medical expenses. The group said they knew that her hospitalization was lasting longer than planned and that a room in the intensive care unit cost more than a regular hospital room, and they wanted to help ensure that Xiao Ting would get all the care she needed. I sent the group a picture of Xiao Ting in her bunny rabbit outfit along with my sincerest appreciation.

A couple of days passed without any communications from Anne, Lizzy, or Holly, so I called Holly. She told me that the officials had come along with the police to inspect the orphanage and interview the people there. At that time they didn't remove any children, but they assured Anne they would return. The children were aware that something was going on but didn't know what. Some of them were old enough to recognize the police uniforms, so maybe they thought somebody was in trouble. Lizzy and Holly had been spending time at the orphanage trying to comfort the children and to help Anne and the workers. On Friday, again not having received any news, I called Anne.

"Ni hao."

"Hello, Anne, this is Jan. How are you and the children?"

"We are not good. Xiao Ting is still very weak, and today the doctors removed her from the ventilator again, and again she failed to keep herself breathing. The doctors said if they hadn't returned her to the ventilator she would have died. Today made the third time she failed to breathe on her own, and the doctors told me they think she will die at the fourth time."

"Oh, I'm so sad to hear that, and I'm sorry for the demands this places on you and your finances as well. Can you see any improvement in her condition? Do you think she is as weak as the doctors say?"

"It seems to me that if the doctors say the surgery was successful in repairing the hole in her heart, then she must be getting stronger on the inside even if we don't see it on the outside. I must believe it, because that is the only hope I have for her."

"Well, I do have some good news for you in regard to the expenses for Xiao Ting's stay in the intensive care unit. The same people who donated the funds for the surgery have given even more money toward her charges for staying in the hospital. In fact, a few other people at our company know about Xiao Ting's operation now and have given some money as well. I wired it to you using the same bank information you gave me when I wired the money for the van. You should have it soon."

"Thank you, and thanks to all of the people helping Xiao Ting. The hospital has been saying something to me every day about the bill and they will be happy to receive a payment from me."

"It's our pleasure to be able to help. I'm also wondering whether the officials returned for another inspection."

"Yes, they came back with the police, and they wanted to see all of my paperwork for the children and any files I had on the computer related to the children. I showed them all of the information I had, and they removed eleven of the children and are taking them back to their home provinces. I begged them not to take my children away, but they were only following their orders."

"Oh no! I've been hoping that wouldn't happen. Too many children! Eleven! I can't imagine what a difference there must be in your home now. Please tell me the other children are okay."

"No, they are not okay. They're very afraid the police will come and take them away too. We don't know whether the officials and police will return or not. It was horrible! The children who were being removed were screaming and crying because they didn't want to leave their home or their friends or me. Some of the children were trying to hide, and the ones who are still here don't know if they will be allowed to stay. Even the children who are from this province are scared because they don't want any additional brothers and sisters removed."

"That must have been a traumatic situation for the children to witness. I'm sorry it happened. How are you holding up?"

"I'm very sad and frustrated, but I can't do anything to stop what is happening. All I can do is be strong for the children and be their mother. It's much quieter at our home now than before. I've had some security cameras installed because if I'm at the hospital with Xiao Ting and someone comes again, I want to know. I'm very, very hopeful that they will not return."

"Do you know where the children who were removed are being taken?"

"Sure. I know which provinces they are from, so I know where they will be placed. I know most of the leaders of the municipal orphanages where the children will go. Maybe one day I can visit them."

"Wow, I know that would be so special for the children to receive a visit from you! What are some of your main concerns for the children who were removed?"

"It's a completely new environment for then. They will have to make new friends and meet new workers, and for those who can go to school, that will be new as well. The main concern I have is the love the children had here, compared to what attention they will receive at their new orphanage. Here, if a child is sick and it's time for one of the workers to go home, they will still stay to take care of the child because they love them and see this as more than a job. At their new orphanages, at three o'clock in the afternoon the workers will be looking at their watches and thinking about getting on a bus to go home. That's the main difference. We love the children here, but I'm afraid they will not be loved as much at the new orphanages."

My respect for Anne continued to grow. I couldn't imagine how she was able to maintain her composure amid all of the stress she faced. Now my thoughts were also with my little friends who had been removed from her home; some of them would be facing new challenges in unfamiliar environments, and all of them had already had a hard life so far. I'm sure some of the children who were removed felt that they were being punished, even though they had done nothing wrong. They were scared and homesick. I knew, though, that they would survive in their new environment no matter how challenging and frightening it may be.

24

THE SECRET

Thankfully I had more candidates to interview in China, so I was able to return almost immediately. With the schedule I had planned, I would be able to stop by and see Holly, Lizzy, Anne, and the children. When I arrived, Holly and Lizzy met me at the bus station. We all went and had lunch together before going to the hospital to see Xiao Ting. When I saw Anne there, I gave her a big hug.

"How is Xiao Ting doing today?" I asked. "Any changes?"

"No changes, and the doctors say they won't try to take her off the ventilator again until next week."

I gazed at Xiao Ting. She was so tiny and still in the bed, yet somehow she seemed on the verge of stirring. "As I look at her," I said, "it seems like her eyes are almost starting to open. What do you think, Lizzy?"

"You are not the first person who has said that, but I see her so often that I don't notice any changes."

I turned to Anne. "At my company, there are so many people now who know about you, the children, and Xiao Ting, that I'm often asked to go to departmental meetings and give everyone an update. I'm thrilled to tell you that many people have wanted to help, so I have more money for you today. I trust this will help with Xiao Ting's medical bills. I believe now I even have enough to cover her stay beyond today!"

"Oh, that is such wonderful news! Every day I owe the hospital more and more for her treatment in the intensive care unit. I will never be able to thank you and your co-workers enough for your generosity!"

"Anne, we are the ones that can't thank you enough for all you have done and continue to do for the children. I can't imagine what their lives would have been like without your providing for them. I'm wondering . . . since you have a worker here to look after Xiao Ting, would you be able to go to your home with Holly, Lizzy, and me? I brought some toys and candy for the children from the States. Hopefully they'll like them."

"Oh, I'm sure they'll like them. And yes, I can go with you. In fact, I brought the van today because I knew all of you would be here. I can drive us back. I've only had it for two days, so I need more practice driving it. Please don't laugh at me!"

When we arrived at the van in the hospital parking lot, it looked just like the one she had wanted. Through the window I could see where the DVD player was folded into the roof. Anne said that one of us had to stay outside the van and help her back out of the parking space because the van was so big. I thought she was kidding, but Lizzy gave me a nod so I knew she was being serious. It was kind of funny watching Anne being so careful, but she was correct: it was difficult to navigate the large van in the confined space of the parking lot. Once we got on the road, Anne's cautioned continued; I doubted she would ever get a speeding ticket.

When we entered the orphanage, we received the same warm greeting as always. The children were smiling and waving their arms in the air. But there were noticeably fewer children. I quickly set my backpack down and pulled out the toys and games.

I sat on the sofa where Xiao Ting used to crawl on to my lap and looked around at the children. The vibe was very different now. The noise level had decreased, and it seemed like the walls gave a slight echo. I couldn't understand how the children could be so resilient. They were so happy to be playing with the new toys and games, and they didn't seem to have a care in the world.

The children's attitudes and energy inspired me to examine myself and consider how stressed I had been lately. Here I was living a dream, with a new job, making more money than I ever could have imagined—and yet I remained exhausted and wound up so tightly that many times I felt on the verge of bursting. Wealth gives you options, and your decisions about what to do with your options say much about your character. Maybe this was all coming full-circle for me. I had initially come to China a few years before to learn to depend on others and become less determined to control things; and I had learned to trust others by putting myself in an environment where I couldn't even get something to eat on my own, due to my lack of language skills. But now I saw that these special needs orphans were teaching me even more. My growing success and financial independence couldn't guarantee happiness for me. Apparently, happiness was a conscious choice I had to make for myself; it would have to come from within. But I wondered how I could find it within myself. If it wasn't there, how could I obtain it? I saw in the children's innocent joy something I would love to have in my own life. Their acceptance of others, regardless of where they were from or what physical challenges they had, was beautiful to see; and I knew I wanted to be like my new little teachers.

25

THE JOURNALIST

When we left Anne's apartment, Holly, Lizzy, and I agreed that it would be nice to catch up with each other for a little while. We decided to stop at one of our favorite coffee places.

"Holly and Lizzy, how's your coffee? Doesn't it smell delicious?"

"Mine is wonderful," Holly said. "How about yours, Lizzy?"

"Darling, I have never met a cup of coffee at this time of day that I didn't love! You know I can use some caffeine in the afternoon for a little pick-me-up."

"I'm glad to hear that I'm not the only one! Okay, I have a good topic for us to discuss since we just left the orphanage and Anne. I had a brief conversation once with Anne about other orphanages she had seen. She told me there was a broad spectrum of facilities, and she gave me a very brief description of a couple of them. She also told me that she hadn't been inside one of the new, large, modern municipal orphanages, so she doesn't know what they were like. Maybe it's just the reporter in me, or perhaps it's my background as an orphan, but I would truly love to see these other orphanages. Holly, since you have so many contacts, do you think you might be able to help me visit some?"

"Well, I have had some exposure to other orphanages, and I do know a few people who work with them. Yes, I think I could help you see additional facilities."

"Wonderful. I knew you would have contacts; you're amazing that way. Lizzy, do you have any other ideas along these lines?"

"No, the only exposure I have had to orphanages in China is the same as yours, so I'm afraid I won't be of any help."

"No problem. So, Holly, do you think you'll be able to arrange for me to see a facility this week?"

"Perhaps, but I will need to make some phone calls to be sure. One independent orphanage I know about is in a rural area north of our city, but the drive isn't too long. I'll check with the director and let you know."

"Oh, that would be wonderful. And this time I insist on paying for the driver. Lizzy, would you care to join us?

"No, I don't think my schedule would permit me to travel with you, but I look forward to learning about what you see."

It was bright and clear the morning we went to visit the municipal orphanage. Holly arrived in a car with a driver I hadn't met before. "Hey, Holly, it's great to see you on this beautiful morning," I said as I slid into the seat beside her. "What can you tell me about the orphanage we're going to see today?"

"It certainly is a grand morning! Well, this orphanage was started by a lady with an amazing story. I don't recall all the details, but she experienced some sort of a miraculous healing when she was actually supposed to die from a disease. After her healing, she became sort of a community leader with a vision to help others. She started the orphanage and grew it to a size far bigger than anyone had anticipated. She also has started a facility to help elderly people supplement their retirement income by cutting hair and working at a restaurant staffed entirely by senior citizens."

"Wow, she sounds like she must have endless energy and great passion for serving others!"

"Yes, I have heard many good things about her, but unfortunately we won't get to meet her today."

"Oh, that's too bad. But I'm still excited to see the orphanage."

"Well, I hate to burst your bubble, but I don't think you will be impressed with this orphanage. You see, their funds are very limited, although they do the best they can for everyone under their care. The community where the orphanage is located is very small and rural, though the neighbors try to help. They are planning to build a nicer facility for the children, but that has led to some arguments in the community. Some want to grow crops on a plot of land and sell those to raise money for a better facility, others want to take out a loan, and still others want to do a fundraiser like a capital campaign."

"Well, it sounds like there are many people who want to help. Surely they'll come together and work it all out for the betterment of the children."

"Let's hope you're correct; but I must also tell you that at this facility they don't only have children."

"What do you mean? It's an orphanage, isn't it?"

"Yes it is, but they have some adults under their care as well. And now they might have fewer children than usual, what with the recent inspections. We'll see when we get there."

About an hour later, our driver pulled into a walled-off industrial area. I wasn't sure whether we were at the right place. Holly pointed to the second floor of a concrete-block building that needed to be painted. "It's up there," she said. The metal stairs going up to the home were rusty, and there was a chicken coop underneath them. In the courtyard outside the orphanage were several large electrical transformers. The driver told Holly that they were currently in use. It was clearly a horrible place for the children to play!

"A husband and wife have been employed to provide care for everyone you will see here. Her name is Deng, and his name is Lee. See! They're motioning for us to come inside."

As we made our way up the rusty stairs, I honestly didn't believe they would support our weight. I knew that if my foot broke through them, I would be cut by the metal and need a tetanus shot immediately.

Deng and Lee greeted us at the entrance with huge smiles, and Lee was holding a little boy. Holly made the introductions for us. Then Deng and Lee gave us a tour of their facility. The entire floor was poorly lit, since the only light in the main room was what came in through the windows. My guess was that they couldn't afford any unnecessary electricity.

We saw a room with sleeping mats on the floor, each with a matching sheet and blanket. The next room down the hall was a dark and sparsely-equipped kitchen. For some reason, the kitchen windows were bricked over. The room was illuminated by three light bulbs hanging from the ceiling on a single strand of wiring.

We crossed the hall to go into the next room. This room was by far the largest room we had seen, and had more light coming through the windows. I noticed about fifteen people sitting around the perimeter of the room. They seemed almost lifeless. Their clothes looked old and were torn in some places, and nobody was wearing the traditional slippers. The children just gazed at the floor when we were being shown around the room (though perhaps that's what they were instructed to do). I didn't understand what Lee and Deng were saying to Holly, but I could tell this must be their playroom because I saw some toys and balls in a box with a cloth partially covering it. Perhaps they had cleaned up the toys in preparation for our visit.

Deng and Lee seemed to truly care for everyone, and everyone sitting around responded to them when they started speaking to them or touching them. Lee seemed especially fond of the club-footed little boy he had been carrying. Holly later told me that Lee couldn't believe someone would abandon such a cute and intelligent boy because of his feet. He was sure the little boy was intelligent, because he paid attention to everything going on around him and loved books.

I pulled Holly to the side and asked, "Do you think they have enough food to eat?"

"Lee told me when we were in the kitchen that some days they don't eat as well as others. He was trying to save face, but I can assure you, they don't buy many groceries. They depend on gifts from others."

"That is so sad. Would it be inappropriate if I gave them some money before we left?"

"They would love that. I was thinking of doing the same thing myself. Let's make sure they have enough to buy food for the rest of the week and to stock their shelves."

"Here's some money. Would you please put that with yours when you give it to them?"

"Certainly. Thanks for your generous nature toward strangers!"

As our tour was ending, Holly gave the couple the money, and we said our good-byes and made our way down the rickety stairs. Once we got in the car, I had so many questions for Holly.

"You know, we talked before about how a child is supposed to leave an orphanage once they reached the age of fourteen. Well, at this orphanage I saw a few people who appeared to be too old to legally be in an orphanage. What do you think is the story with that?"

"You're correct; the facility does house a few people who are clearly older than fourteen. They also appeared to be suffering from depression."

"Yeah, they looked so sad to me. They almost seemed comatose. I only saw physical problems like cleft pallet, clubfoot, and spina bifida at Anne's orphanage, so seeing the older people there who seemed depressed was a surprise to me. Would you tell me some of the things Deng and Lee were saying to you?"

"They were saying that some of the people who wanted to contribute to the orphanage, by selling vegetables or other means, don't like them, because sometimes they put children in the sidecar of their motorcycle and take them to a location where they can ask people to give money for the children. You may have noticed the red motorcycle when we walked past it. Deng and Lee were desperate for money, so they were doing anything they could to provide for everyone. I can't fault them for trying."

It was hard to imagine an orphanage having so few resources, but I had heard such sad stories before. I asked Holly about one of them. "One of the ladies who worked in the office at the university told me she had heard that sometimes there are so many babies in an orphanage that the workers don't have time to hold them. The demands on the workers' time is so great that, rather than holding the babies to feed them, they put each baby's bottle in a mechanical arm that is positioned over the baby's mouth. She said that when a baby is new and still has a soft head, if the baby isn't picked up often enough and just lies in bed all the time, the head will become flat in the back. Have you ever seen that happening?"

"I agree that sometimes the workers must feel overwhelmed by the number and needs of the babies, but I have never seen a mechanical arm for feeding a baby."

"That certainly is good to hear. Babies need a lot of touching to thrive."

Holly quoted the Chinese philosopher Mengzi to me: "All the children who are held and loved will know how to love others . . . Spread these virtues in the world. Nothing more need be done."

I thought about this for a few moments. "Wow, those are words of wisdom indeed, and much deeper than they appear at the surface."

Holly agreed. "China has been blessed to have many wise thinkers from whose words we can learn. Speaking of learning, I know you have a limited amount of time in China this trip, so I tentatively made arrangements for us to visit another facility a few hours south of here. Can you do that today? If so, I'll call them and let them know we're coming."

"Yes, I can do that, and I appreciate your consideration of my travel schedule. What can you tell me about this other facility?"

"Well, it's very different from the one we just saw. Their financial situation is significantly better. The family that started this orphanage is from the States. They adopted a little girl from China, and when their adoptive daughter became an adult, she persuaded her parents to start an orphanage in the rural area where she was born. The parents have a successful business in the States, so they and a few of their friends and business associates have funded this orphanage."

"I'm impressed that the young woman wanted to be connected with her homeland in a special way."

"Yes, she's quite active with the operations of the orphanage, and she spends a considerable amount of time in the States raising funds for it."

"Will we meet her today?"

"I'm afraid we won't, but I'm sure you'll be impressed with this orphanage. We have a significant drive ahead of us, so to break it up, I know of a wonderful noodle restaurant I'm sure you will enjoy."

"Holly, you never cease to amaze me with your contacts and your knowledge of the area. A bowl of noodles sounds great to me!"

After a delicious lunch at the restaurant, where Holly knew the owner (as usual), we drove for what seemed like a lot longer than Holly had initially indicated. The roads were narrow and poorly maintained, but the scenery was wonderful. Just when I thought the conditions couldn't get any worse, we turned onto a dirt road. The driver's GPS was going crazy. After a very bumpy few miles, Holly admitted that she didn't know where we were, so we stopped and asked a farmer how to locate the orphanage. Because the dirt roads weren't marked, we stopped at least two more times to seek assistance with our directions. Finally, Holly and the driver felt we were very close. We turned onto yet another dirt road that led us up an incline, until we could finally see some buildings in the distance. The brush lining the road was well maintained, and the road itself had fewer ruts. As we rounded a curve, the dirt road became a concrete road, and we were very close to the buildings.

The view from here was spectacular. An enormous pasture below us looked like it went on for miles. At the end of it was a stand of trees, and beyond them in the distance was a very large lake. I doubted that all of the land belonged to the orphanage, but they certainly had a prime location for a view.

We exited the car and a lady came to meet us. She and Holly had a conversation as I took in the surroundings. Holly gave the introductions and translated our greetings, then we walked a little farther up the hill and entered a large building. Beyond the spacious entrance was a large open room with children and workers everywhere. One child was doing gymnastics in the middle of the room and was funny to watch. He was full of life and energy, and laughed loudly when he fell down. Near the door where we entered was a lady cutting hair. The little boy getting his hair cut was not cooperating, so another worker was holding him and encouraging him to be still. Many children were sitting on furniture and on the floor, watching a DVD. The room had a very clean checkerboard tile floor, but it seemed to me that the space as a whole could have used more light.

Beyond the open area was a hall with a few large bedrooms, and beyond that were the bathrooms. Apparently it was bath time, because children were enjoying running around the large open room, wrapped up in large towels. Unfortunately for some of them, they had to get in line for haircuts. The workers seemed to love and enjoy the children greatly.

We exited the large building, and went into one of the smaller buildings across the driveway. This was the laundry building, and several industrial-sized washers were running. I couldn't imagine how many loads of laundry needed to be done here daily, but I was certain it was a constant need. The next building we visited was the dining hall. Part of this building was a screened-in porch with picnic tables, and inside were more tables in a very large open area. The big room definitely had the feel of a cafeteria (complete with a stainless steel serving line and trays for carrying food to the table). The workers in the kitchen all wore hats or hairnets, and looked to be cleaning up after lunch service had ended. The walls were a bright yellow, and it was better illuminated than the others.

Our next area to tour was a well-equipped and maintained playground situated on a grassy slope. I didn't see any weeds growing in the playground area, and there were many different pieces of equipment for the children to play on. The little boy who was doing the gymnastics routine in the first building must have loved playing on the jungle gym equipment.

We crossed back over the driveway and went to another large building, which was used as both an office and a residence for the woman from the States when she was in town. This building, unlike any of the others, had curtains. The desks in the office were piled high with papers, envelopes, and office equipment.

As we started making our way back down the driveway to the car, Holly stopped a couple of times and spoke with the woman who was leading our tour. Finally we all shook hands, and Holly and I got in the car to leave.

I had a very positive feeling about this facility. "Holly, you were right. I definitely prefer this orphanage to the first one we toured. Please tell me all that you learned from the tour guide."

"Well, the buildings we didn't tour are either like the large one with bedrooms and bathrooms that we already saw, or they are smaller ones used for storage. One more building is a medical office."

"Wow, that is impressive that they have a designated space for medical attention. What else is there for me to know?"

"Let's see. They have fifty-seven children living there, and some of them are completely healthy; they just need a forever home and family. Other children have varying degrees of illness or special needs, which you saw firsthand in the large building we visited. Many of the children were at school, so that's why we didn't go into the other large dormitories. The tour guide also told me that all of the land you see in the view going down to the lake belongs to the orphanage."

"Wow, that's amazing that they purchased so much land. The founders of the orphanage made a fantastic decision with the location."

"I agree with you. The view is breathtaking, and they have unlimited opportunities to expand if they want to. By the way, the local people are so pleased with the orphanage and its founders that most of the workers there are volunteers. The only paid workers are the main cook, a couple of office workers, the nurse, a couple of the groundskeepers, and some of the leaders of the dormitories."

"It's wonderful to see a community coming together like that. In all of my travels in China, I must say that I consistently encounter kindhearted people."

"I'm glad you like this facility and feel you have been treated well by the Chinese. And I have a surprise for you for tomorrow!"

26

IMMACULATE

My surprise was that Holly had arranged to travel with me to Beijing, where I was to conduct more interviews, and for us to visit another orphanage outside the city. Because we both had business in Beijing, the timing was excellent for us.

Our journey was pleasant. We had one conversation after another with fellow passengers, and I was thankful Holly was willing to translate for me. After the train ride, we took a taxi to our hotel, checked in, and unpacked in no time at all. Holly then called our driver, and he was already waiting for us in the lobby. She seemed to know drivers everywhere she went.

It was hard to tell where Beijing stopped and the next city started during our trip to the orphanage. Holly had said that I would be impressed by this facility, and that was a huge understatement. My eyes grew large as we passed through the gates, and Holly laughed. "See, I thought you would be impressed!"

"Wow, Holly, the grounds are amazing! Look at how they used the plants to make patterns in the ground. Now that takes talent and time! All of the buildings look so new, clean, and modern. I can't wait to see inside the buildings and hear the stories."

"An American named Matt will be showing us around, so I won't have to do any translating for you like at the other orphanages. You will be able to ask any questions you like."

"What is an American doing at this orphanage? I didn't expect you to say there was one here, because the buildings look so Chinese in style."

"You see, this orphanage was started by a very successful European business leader. He and his family had adopted a little boy from China, and his business travels brought him back here frequently. He later decided to start an orphanage. Initially, he and his company purchased the land and built the first few buildings. Then he got his business contacts and various companies from all around the world to contribute. Now you can see what that type of financial support can do for an orphanage in China. The founder doesn't travel here much, but he hired Matt to direct the orphanage."

We saw signs in many languages telling visitors where to go, and each building was labeled as well. When we approached the office, a man came out to greet us.

"Hey Holly, great to see you again. Hopefully you had an enjoyable trip."

"Matt, it is always a pleasure to see you, and thanks for your willingness to give us a tour on such short notice. This is my friend Jan, whom I told you about. She's already impressed by your facility."

"Nice to meet you, Jan, and welcome to our orphanage. Hopefully you'll still be impressed when you have completed the tour!"

"Nice to meet you too, Matt. If the interior of these buildings are half as nice as the exterior, I will be very impressed indeed."

"If you don't mind me asking you, Jan, what has caught your eye so far?"

"Well, you have a gate and the buildings are enclosed by walls, so I would say you are very security conscious. Your grounds are beautiful and well laid out, so I would say someone has an eye for detail. It looks like you have kept the traditional architecture with the roofline going out to a point on every corner, and the buildings look like they were painted this morning, so you must have a great staff working here. The windows are significantly larger than what I see in most buildings like this, and I'm guessing that they let in lots of natural light. How am I doing so far?"

"Maybe it is you who has an eye for details, Jan! I don't think I need to tell you to keep your eyes open for special things we have done to make the children happy and comfortable here—so let's get started. On the other side of this office building is one of the buildings housing the children."

On the sidewalk, smooth rocks were protruding slightly enough from the concrete to be noticeable, so I had to ask why. Matt said, "Holly, why don't you answer that one for me, since I am sure you know more about it than I do."

"Jan," Holly said, "you know how you see so many foot massage places around China? Well, that's because we believe that much of your health involves your feet. When you walk on the rocks, it's like you're getting a foot massage and thus improving your health."

Matt entered a code into a number pad next to the front door of a large building. He turned to me and explained, "Jan, you were right when you said we are security conscious. With this system we can track every time a door is opened, and we know who opened it because everyone has a different code."

We entered into a very large room with a spotlessly clean tile floor and a large rug covering much of it. There must have been thirty children playing in this room, and all of them wore nice clothes. Several workers were in the room attending to the children. We sat on sofas and overstuffed chairs, and played with the children. The children came to us with no trepidation, so I knew they were accustomed to seeing foreigners and strangers.

On the way upstairs, we passed an area for washing clothes. At each end of the hallway was a gate to prevent anyone from playing on the stairs or falling down them. On the second floor we entered a room with mats on the floor, where a couple of workers were doing what looked like physical therapy with a few of the children. The room also had many beds with rails to keep the children from falling out of bed.

"We put the children who can't walk, or who can't walk very well, upstairs because they will be less likely to want to play on the stairs. Hopefully we will prevent injuries by doing this. Since making this decision, we haven't had any children fall, but one worker did fall when her foot was caught in some sheets she was carrying downstairs for the laundry."

"Oh, I'm sorry to hear about that. Is she okay?"

"She injured her wrist, and had some bruises on her arms and knees, but avoided any serious injuries. Speaking of the stairs, let's go back down, and I'll show you more of the building."

We went down the stairs and followed the hall to the right. Matt showed us the restrooms, which were quite large and had tile walls for easy cleaning. He also showed us the bedrooms full of nice, sturdy furniture.

"Let's visit our dining hall next to see the workers preparing a meal."

"Matt," I asked, "how do you decide which child lives in which building?"

"Good question, Jan. There are many factors we take into consideration. First and foremost, we always keep family members together. Next we evaluate the amount of care each child will need. Age is also a consideration. When particular children seem to have great relationships with each other, we try to keep them together. That seems to be especially important for the older girls. Conversely, if certain children don't play well together and we can't correct the problem, we'll try to separate them. But we don't need to do that very often."

We entered the dining hall, and Matt spread his arms proudly. "As you can see, we can accommodate many children at one sitting. The food here is quite good, and we have a dietitian and many wonderful cooks on staff. We have a couple of vans and drivers who stay busy picking up the food we need, getting parts for the maintenance department, and running errands when they arise. The cooks and the dietitian will fuss at the drivers if they bring back food that doesn't meet their standards. But everyone knows the drivers do their best to select the highest quality produce they can."

"The size of your rice cookers reminds me of the ones in the cafeterias on our university's campus," I observed. "All of the stainless steel bowls remind me of the food line at a bus stop, too. How many children live here?"

"Jan, we have 178 children living here currently, but this Saturday two of them will be relocated for adoption. It will be a bittersweet day for us. We want to see as many children as possible get adopted, but we do grow to love them while they are here. Now let me show you the guest dormitory."

We exited the dining hall and walked through a lovely flower garden to reach the next large building. It was longer and narrower than the other buildings, and with good reason: a long hallway led to multiple bedrooms, some with bunk beds and some with a single queen-size bed. All of the bedrooms had their own bathroom, and each bathroom was supplied with a hair dryer. The center of the building had a den with an enormous large-screen TV. There was also a sitting room, a computer room, and a meeting room.

"Matt, sorry for all of the questions, but why do you need a guest house when you are completely staffed? By the way, this is another impressive building."

"No problem, Jan. Holly told me you would ask many questions, so I was prepared." We all laughed before Matt continued. "We have individuals and groups who like to come and volunteer here, and we even have medical teams that come and provide medical care for the children, so we want to give them a nice place to stay, since they are being so generous to us. In fact, if you look out these windows, the next building you see is designated as a gym for our guests. We have weights, elliptical machines, treadmills, a sauna, and an indoor pool for them in that building. Now let's go to the office, because I have something for you there."

The office was by far the smallest building we entered, but it was just as nicely furnished and maintained as the other buildings. I don't know how the maintenance workers kept the walls so clean. I didn't see a scuff or any chipped paint the entire day.

"We have a small reception area in the office where we have a little snack and drink that were prepared for both of you. Holly, I remember you don't eat many sweets, so we have some salty snacks for you. And Jan, please help yourself to whatever you prefer."

We gathered our snacks and sat at the table. "Tell me something, Matt. Is this orange juice freshly squeezed? It's amazing!"

"Yes, Jan. It was squeezed about fifteen minutes ago by one of our kitchen workers. The cookies were baked here at about the same time. Now do you have any more questions before you leave?"

"I couldn't help noticing that a new building is going up about seventy yards away. What will that be?"

"That will be another dormitory for the children. We are expanding our housing capacity because we want to help additional children."

"Now *that* is a wonderful goal. Believe it or not, I can't think of any more questions just now. Thanks so much for your time today!"

"Oh, you're welcome." Matt stood, and we stood with him. "Holly, it is always a pleasure to see you again. And Jan, here is my business card. Please don't hesitate to contact me if I can serve you."

"Thanks, Matt. I may reach out to you one day."

We enjoyed a pleasant ride back to the hotel, but there was something I had to know from Holly. "How do you know all of the people who lead these orphanages?"

"Actually, I don't know them that well, and I don't know Deng and Lee at all. But since I was once the Dean of the Foreign Language Department, I've had a few books published, and I speak both Chinese and English fluently, so sometimes I'm asked to help foreigners with formal documents like contracts. That's how I met Matt. We really don't know each other well, but we've stayed in touch."

"When I'm with you, I feel as though I'm with a rock star! Do you have any other hidden talents that have helped you attract so many friends and contacts?"

"No, I'm not an overly talented person, but I do try to use the skills I have to help others. Now before we say good-bye, I want make sure I haven't left you with the wrong impression about the care of orphans in China. Yes, I have been exposed to many foreigners helping the orphans here, but there are many Chinese providing wonderful services to orphans as well. Together, the Chinese and foreigners make a passionate team in caring for the children."

"Holly, you are always my teacher, and thanks for that reminder. I'm thankful that you were able to introduce me to a broad range of facilities. All of these orphanages will be on my mind while I conduct my interviews and complete the other work David requested for this trip. Then I'm flying straight back to the States from Beijing. It might be a while before I see you again."

"As usual, Jan, I'm thankful for the time we've spent together and for the assistance you've given to our little friends. I'll be departing early tomorrow morning because I have a driver transporting me to visit some classmates between here and home, so I don't think I'll see you before I go."

"I'll miss you as always, Holly, and I'll stay in touch after I get home." We gave each other a quick hug and then returned to our rooms to prepare for our afternoon meetings.

27

HALLELUJAH

I was back home in the States, and settling in for a morning of catching up with my teams, when a call came through from China.

"Jan, this is Anne. I have some wonderful news for you. The doctors removed Xiao Ting from the ventilator, and she is breathing on her own! It has been exactly thirty days—one month—and finally she can breathe all by herself."

"Awesome! That is the best news I have received in a month! What do the doctors say about her condition?"

"They think in time she will have a full recovery. She is still weak, but she doesn't need the ventilator anymore."

"Wow, and those are the same doctors who told you multiple times they didn't think she would survive!"

"They don't know how long she'll need to be in the hospital, but she'll be removed from the intensive care unit today!"

"Man, that is just such great news. I can't wait to tell my friends at work!"

"I have additional good news for you. I've arranged to travel to the other provinces to visit the children who were removed from my home."

"That's great news, too! I'm so glad you'll get to see them."

"Well, I know you have work to do. I'll let you know how Xiao Ting progresses and how the trip goes."

"Great. I appreciate all you're doing for the children, and thanks for letting me know your fantastic news."

Even through my intense jet lag I felt a burst of energy and euphoria. I quickly sent an email update to all who had been interested in Xiao Ting and the children at the orphanage. I knew Mark's team was having a meeting that afternoon, so I rushed out and picked up some cookies and cupcakes so we could celebrate her successful removal from the ventilator. It truly was a joyous and sincere meeting that day. Mark was gracious enough to let me take a few minutes of the meeting time to thank everyone again for their support, and some indicated that they wanted to continue supporting our friends at Anne's.

28

REUNITED

The fact that Anne wanted to go visit the children who were formerly in her care spoke volumes about her deep love and concern for them. The results of the trip were stunning.

When Anne visited Lily, the little girl we had lost in the park, she was told that Lily had become unmanageable for the employees of the new orphanage. The workers thought Lily's developmental and vision issues were worsening, and that—combined with her unhappiness at being there—was consuming a disproportionate amount of the workers' time. Anne explained that Lily hadn't been a problem at her orphanage, so she suggested that she take Lily back. The leader of the new orphanage agreed that it might be best for Lily, the workers, and children at his orphanage if she returned to Anne, so they drew on all of the relationships that could help Anne to adopt Lily quickly. The final approval was put on the paperwork that day, and she was able to take Lily home with her. Now that Anne has legally adopted her, she can never be removed from Anne's care again.

At a different orphanage, Anne heard some heartbreaking news about Meng He, the boy with the burn scars. When Anne visited, Meng He told her that on three different occasions he had gone three days without eating. Anne asked if they were giving him food, and he said he was given food, but he didn't feel like eating. He said that in his heart he was counting each day he was away from her, and that the day of her visit was day thirty-three. Anne immediately went to the officials and inquired about adopting Meng He, because she knew that the best environment for him was at her home. She loved him dearly, and couldn't bear the thought of him being so upset and homesick that he wouldn't eat.

Anne was able to quickly adopt Meng He as well. Maybe it was permitted because everyone was concerned about his well-being, or because the new orphanage was overcrowded after receiving so many children. Meng He didn't understand all that was being said in the office about his adoption, nor did he understand any of the papers being signed and made official; but when Anne walked out of the office with him and told him that she had legally adopted him, and that he could never be taken away again, he jumped up and down, then hugged her as strongly as he could with his thin arms. As they embraced each other, tears were streaming down both of their faces.

I am so thankful that the government allowed Anne to adopt Lily and Meng He, because now the children will be in a loving and comfortable environment where they can mature and thrive for many years to come.

Unfortunately the same wonderful news doesn't apply for Xiao Ting. At first everything was going well. Her operation was successful, and after some time she was well enough to return to Anne's. A family from near my hometown in the States was waiting to adopt her once she was released from the hospital. They had initiated the process, with the paperwork and home inspections, but then Xiao Ting's status changed.

Anne received a call from Xiao Ting's home province indicating that they wanted Xiao Ting back under their care, just like so many other children who had been removed from Anne's care after the horrible fire in the independent orphanage. Anne explained to the officials in the other province that Xiao Ting was too weak to travel, so she would need to stay with her to fully recover from the operation. For many months Anne was able to prevent the officials from reclaiming her, but ultimately, Anne knew she would have to let her go. In the meantime, she worked on the documentation necessary for Xiao Ting to be adopted, and she made sure all of the health paperwork was in order. It was a sad day indeed when our little Xiao Ting was removed from Anne's loving care.

Although Xiao Ting was finally healthy and could travel, even on a long flight back to the States to the family who wanted to adopt her, it sadly never happened. The staff at the new orphanage assured Anne that they had completed the paperwork for Xiao Ting's adoption, but something fell through. Periodically Anne calls and speaks to Xiao Ting and checks on her progress, and she is thriving. The surgery we raised money for has given her a new chance for a long and healthy life.

Note from the Author:
THEY NEED YOU

Although this book is fictional, the story is based on what I have seen, heard, smelled, felt, and experienced during my time in China. Anne and her orphanage are real, but the names have been altered to protect the identities of the children and staff. The real Anne is very protective of her little ones, and I am thankful for her tenacity! I would love to share their playful, affectionate, sweet, and loving faces with you; but to protect their privacy, I am sharing only their stories.

As I think about my involvement with the children at Anne's orphanage, I am amazed by the joy they have, even with their limitations and circumstances. I continuously think about how easy it is for me to get on a plane and go visit them, and put a smile on their faces with just a little attention. This has led me to start a non-profit organization called Global Partners in Life, so I can create a larger circle of people dedicated to helping with the children's care. Global Partners in Life provides for the educational, humanitarian, and medical needs of orphans—particularly special needs orphans—in China.

I feel extraordinarily blessed to play a small part in the lives of these children, and it is an honor each time I am in their presence.

The surgeries we have provided for some of the children have saved their lives, and for others they have greatly increased their quality of life—not just for one day, but for many years into the future.

There are orphans all around the world, many of them with special needs. Some of them receive wonderful care, but some are living in deplorable conditions. The reality is that if you invest your time, talent, and resources, these children can have much happier and healthier lives. You can get involved with Global Partners in Life or with one of the many other local and international organizations that help orphans. You might also consider being a foster parent or adopting children, and opening your home and arms to someone who desperately needs you. Maybe you'll even decide to start your own nonprofit to help orphans. If you do, please let me know and I'd be happy to help.

The children who are on my heart are in China. Where are the children who are on your heart?

———

One day an elephant saw a hummingbird lying on its back with its tiny feet up in the air.

"What are you doing?" asked the elephant.

The hummingbird replied, "I heard that the sky might fall today, so I am ready to help hold it up, should it fall."

The elephant laughed cruelly. "Do you really think that those tiny feet could help hold up the sky?"

The hummingbird kept his feet up in the air, intent on his purpose, as he replied, "Not alone. But each must do what he can. And this is what I can do."

—*A Chinese Folktale*

ACKNOWLEDGEMENTS

It is very humbling to take on a task when you are not skilled or experienced, and that is the situation I found myself in when I wanted to write about the children in China. Fortunately, Becky Robinson and her amazing team at Weaving Influence came to my side for assistance! They knew what needed to be done, when to do it, and, most importantly, how to do it very well. For any aspect of the publishing process, I could depend on Becky and Weaving Influence to address the challenges with experienced and gifted people.

A special thank you goes to the wonderful people serving orphans in China, especially Anne and her staff. You welcomed a foreigner into your home and shared your lives with me as well as sharing the needs of the children. You have allowed me into your home and lives countless times, and I am very grateful for your openness toward me.

The children we serve and provide for have welcomed and accepted me as their friend, even though I am much older and a foreigner. They have taught me about acceptance of others, acceptance of your life situation, and finding joy in life. We have played together and yes, even grown up together, and they have offered me many special moments in my life. I thank them for all their greetings and welcoming smiles when we meet.

This book would never have been written, or even considered, if it were not for Mark Miller, author of *Chess Not Checkers* and coauthor of the international bestseller *The Secret*. Mark leads a men's leadership group, which I have been part of for at least seventeen years. I have always been impressed with him as an excellent model of what he teaches: servant leadership. Additionally, Mark serves on the Board of Directors for Global Partners in Life (GPiL), the non-profit organization which supports the work being done with orphans in China. It was a challenge from Mark to me that led to the writing of this book.

I must thank my parents, John and Claudette Sides, who provided a loving home for my sister, Toni, and me, in which we grew up. This gave me an understanding view of what type of an environment my new friends, the orphans in China, needed.

I have never known anyone that truly cares for others (with either two or four legs!) as much as my loving wife, Leah. Thank you, Leah. My nickname for you, "Pieshell," is perfect, because like a pie's shell, you are beautiful; and also like a pie, the best part is on the inside, which is your heart. Your compassion for others, which I see you demonstrate frequently, is a quality I try to replicate as I strive to assist the orphans in China. Thank you for your support of starting GPiL and for your understanding of all of my trips and time in China. I have learned there is no value that can be placed on a wonderful spouse!

ABOUT THE AUTHOR

Beau Sides, humanitarian and author of *Lessons from China: A Westerner's Cultural Education*, is the Founder and President of Global Partners in Life (GPiL), a 501c3 non-profit organization that helps children through young adults with educational, humanitarian, and medical needs in China. The focus of GPiL is orphans and special needs orphans.

As a former IBM manager, Beau combined his business acumen, leadership skills, and passion for serving others to form GPiL in 2004. Today, the organization celebrates eleven years of serving for the purpose of enabling young lives to prosper.

For Beau, each opportunity to assist or provide for the needs of a child that is truly needy and dependent on others is unique and rewarding. He has enjoyed watching his "little friends" grow over the years, and he hopes to provide a better environment and more resources for them. After almost fifty trips and numerous teaching tours in China, he considers this beautiful country his second home. Beau and his lovely wife, Leah, celebrate twenty-eight years of marriage, and they love and nurture two family dogs.

Connect with Beau on social media:

www.beausides.com

@BeauSides

facebook.com/beausidesauthor

linkedin.com/in/beausides

Made in the USA
Charleston, SC
14 August 2015